Keeping Christmas

Keeping Christmas

Finding Joy in a Season of Excess and Strife

by James A. Hopwood

RESOURCE *Publications* • Eugene, Oregon

KEEPING CHRISTMAS
Finding Joy in a Season of Excess and Strife

Copyright © 2019 James A. Hopwood. All rights reserved. Except for brief quotations in critical publications or reviews, no part of this book may be reproduced in any manner without prior written permission from the publisher. Write: Permissions, Wipf and Stock Publishers, 199 W. 8th Ave., Suite 3, Eugene, OR 97401.

Resource Publications
An Imprint of Wipf and Stock Publishers
199 W. 8th Ave., Suite 3
Eugene, OR 97401

www.wipfandstock.com

PAPERBACK ISBN: 978-1-5326-9537-7
HARDCOVER ISBN: 978-1-5326-9538-4
EBOOK ISBN: 978-1-5326-9539-1

Manufactured in the U.S.A.   AUGUST 14, 2019

Unless noted otherwise, all Scripture quotations are from the New Revised Standard Version Bible, copyright © 1989 National Council of the Churches of Christ in the United States of America. Used by permission. All rights reserved worldwide.

For Linda and Jenny and Erica, who show me the real Christmas.

Contents

Introduction | ix

Chapter One—Two Christmases | 1
Chapter Two—Why December 25? | 21
Chapter Three—Old Style/New Style | 41
Chapter Four—Redeeming the Season | 59
Chapter Five—Christmas Wishes | 78
Chapter Six—The December Dilemma | 98
Chapter Seven—A Blessed Christmas | 116

Endnotes | 123
Bibliography | 127

Introduction

It was said of Ebenezer Scrooge that he knew how to keep Christmas well, if anyone did. But Charles Dickens only hinted at *how* Scrooge kept the holiday well, leaving generations of readers of *A Christmas Carol* to wonder how they might go about it themselves.

This book is about keeping Christmas well. By "keeping" Christmas, I mean not only observing the season with all its joys, but also learning to embrace its many frustrations and guarding it from further encroachment by those who want to use it to promote their own political and social agendas.

In these contentious times, I am especially thinking of those strident voices that are incessantly chattering about a "war on Christmas." Sorry, culture warriors. *There is no war on Christmas.* There is only a war *over* Christmas. Some people want to seize Christmas and use it for their own purposes. There is nothing new here. People have been fighting over Christmas for nearly 1,700 years.

During these seventeen centuries, there *have* been occasional wars *on* Christmas. The most successful of these was waged 350 years ago—and it was waged not by secular forces but by Christians. The Puritans of England and America did such a number on Christmas that though it *did* bounce back from the Puritan onslaught, it never quite recovered, and echoes of the fray continue to reverberate through today's debates.

A few contemporary Grinches *would* like to do away with Christmas altogether, but they don't have much influence, and their importance should not be exaggerated. The real war today, as it has been for most of the 1,700-year struggle, is over *how* Christmas should be celebrated. Whatever "side" they are on, the combatants in this struggle pose the same question: Shall we celebrate *our* way or the *wrong* way?

Introduction

If you want to keep Christmas well, you need to decide the best way for you and your family to celebrate and then shield that vision from those who want to impose their vision on you. How you celebrate Christmas is mostly *your* concern, not the concern of others. And how others celebrate Christmas is mostly *their* concern, not yours.

Before we move on, I should offer a quick advisory. I am a committed follower of Jesus Christ and a retired United Methodist pastor. This book is written from a progressive Christian perspective. If you don't want to hear a Christian perspective, or a perspective that may challenge your sectarian views, perhaps you should stop reading now.

* * *

Christmas is my favorite season of the year. I love the carols, and the decorations, and the sense of expectancy, and the infectious spirit of love and goodwill that seems to touch even the grouchiest of souls.

At the same time, I almost dread the season's approach every year. It's too busy. It's too commercial. It's often venal. How many gifts do we give not out of love or kindness but out of obligation or even guilt?

Every year I say to myself, "This Christmas will be different. This year, we'll celebrate it *right*." But how many times have I packed away the Christmas decorations feeling not a sense of joy but a sense of loss, for again having failed to feel the presence of Christ renewed within me?

Don't you sometimes feel the same way? Don't you wish for that "perfect Christmas"? Is this merely a silly sentimental urge, a tug of nostalgia for a simpler time that never existed? Or is it a yearning that is deeply seated and vital? Can't we celebrate Christmas *better* than we do?

I think we can, and if we don't at least try, I think we are shortchanging ourselves, our families and our God.

This book is a product of my personal spiritual journey. It reflects research into the origins and history of Christmas and reflection on why we do some of the things we do and what that means for us. I do not expect that you always will arrive at the same conclusions that I have, but it is my hope and prayer that these thoughts will help illuminate your search for answers as together we seek ways to better celebrate the birth of Jesus.

Our journey begins with a survey of the cultural battleground called Christmas. Chapter 1, "Two Christmases," looks at the cultural divide that shapes how we think about all things Christmas.

Introduction

- There are two Christmases. One is sacred. One is secular. The Christian holy day and the winter holiday share a common ground, and this is where most of the fighting over Christmas occurs.

Chapter 2 asks "Why December 25?" Here we explore the origins of the cultural divide in the history of Christmas and turn up two very different stories of how and why Christmas was created.

- It is popular, but false, to say that Christmas is a pagan holiday with a Christian veneer. Christians did not steal the holiday from pagans. However, many Christmas traditions do have pagan influences.

Chapter 3, "Old Style/New Style," looks at how people have coped with the cultural split over the centuries and how their contributions to the celebration of the season have made it such a rich blend of contradictory impulses.

- Jesus is the reason for the season, but Jesus is not central to the way the season is widely celebrated and has not been for a long time.

Chapter 4, "Redeeming the Season," asks whether Christmas can be saved, and if so, how.

- Many of the things that make Christmas joyous for most of us have nothing to do with celebrating the birth of Jesus. Yet Christmas without these things would not be the Christmas that we know and cherish. It helps if we view the conflict over Christmas as a reflection of God's incarnation in Jesus. Christmas is a mess because God's involvement in the world is messy business.

The next two chapters focus on specific problems. Chapter 5, "Christmas Wishes," looks at gift giving traditions, especially those involving that fat man in the red suit.

- The celebration of Christmas can get in the way of Jesus' rebirth in our hearts. The bright lights of Christmas can distract us from the true Light, so that Jesus is stillborn rather than reborn in us.

Chapter 6, "The December Dilemma," looks at how the cultural battle plays out in the public sphere.

- Everyone wants a joyous Christmas, but people disagree on what makes Christmas joyful. If you want a joyful Christmas, you have to

INTRODUCTION

invent it for yourself and fend off those who want to impose their political agendas on you.

Finally, Chapter 7 offers ideas on how you can find "A Blessed Christmas," if truly that is your goal.

- Nobody is going to hand you a simpler Christmas. If you want a more meaningful holiday, you have to make it yourself. It's time to reinvent Christmas, again. Maybe we can get it right this time. At least we can try.

Chapter One

Two Christmases

When I say the word "Christmas," do you hear sleigh bells and the clack of reindeer hooves? Or do you hear angelic choruses and the faint cry of a newborn child? When I say the word "Christmas," does your mind's eye envision a Victorian lane where snow is glistening, or the dark streets of a little town where hope streams out from a stable?

When you think of Christmas, do you picture evergreen trees with bright lights or a star shining in the night sky? Do you think of crackling fires, roasting chestnuts and warm drinks, or of shepherds watching their flocks by night? Do you think of ribbons and bows and brightly wrapped gifts, or an infant wrapped in swaddling clothes lying in a manger?

Or do all of these images, and more, flood your senses when you hear the word "Christmas"? And isn't it confusing, sometimes, when the images start to run together in your head?

Someone once gave me a little porcelain Nativity scene that shows Santa Claus on his knees worshipping the Babe in the Manger. I find myself feeling strangely ambivalent about that image. I'm just not sure what to make of it. I think it's trying to say that Jesus is the reason for the season and that even Santa bows before him. But that's simply not true. Santa may be based on a saintly figure, but in popular culture he has no connection with the Baby Jesus. When was the last Santa movie, TV special or coloring book you saw that even *mentioned* Jesus? No, Santa does not bow before Jesus. He stands tall in his sleigh and pounds his chest and pronounces *himself* king of Christmas.

Of *one* Christmas he *is* king. Santa rules over the cultural Christmas. This is the commercial Christmas, which is so focused on the buying and giving of expensive gifts. This is the secular Christmas, celebrating the cheerful optimism of early winter, when the first snows can be so picturesque and delightful. This is the family Christmas, when everyone gathers at grandma's house and tries to set aside grudges that they have carried since childhood. But Santa has very little to do with that *other* Christmas, the one that celebrates the incarnation of God in frail human flesh. You can celebrate *that* Christmas with gifts, winter fun and gatherings at grandma's house. But you can't celebrate it without thinking of Jesus, whose life gives meaning to all the rest.

For Christians, Christmas without Jesus is unthinkable. But for many others, Christmas has nothing to do with Jesus. That cultural divide is crucial to our understanding of Christmas past, present and future.

THE TWO CHRISTMASES

There are two Christmases. One is secular. The other is sacred. One is cultural. The other is Christian. One is a winter holiday. The other is a religious holy day. Although there is some overlap between the two days in timing and tradition and meaning, the two Christmases are in essence very different.

The cultural Christmas is a long winter party that celebrates the warmth of family and friends. Santa Claus is the figurehead of this Christmas. One of the main themes of the season is excess. (You get gifts from a jolly fat man dressed in red with white fur trim. Think about it.)

The sacred Christmas celebrates the incarnation of God in Jesus Christ. The central figure of this Christmas is an infant lying in a bed of hay in a feed box. This Christmas celebrates the birth of hope in a dreary world. It is the kind of hope that no winter party can ever create, no matter how excessive it is or how long it lasts.

There is some overlap between the two Christmases in timing. Together, they form a six-week-long bridge between one year and the next.

The cultural Christmas starts early on the day after Thanksgiving. This day is widely known as Black Friday because the profits made then are said to put so many businesses into the black for the year. (Think of this as National Shopping Day.) In the minds of many people, the season continues until the stroke of midnight on December 25. However, other observers say the season extends to the day *after* Christmas (a.k.a. National Gift Return Day), and even until the first weekend after Christmas. (You know that it's really, finally, *over* when children go back to school, parents go back to work, and rush-hour traffic returns to normal.)

According to the Christian sacred calendar, what begins shortly after Thanksgiving is the season of Advent. Advent is a time of spiritual preparation for the coming of Jesus. Partly, it's a time of preparation for the celebration of Jesus' birth on that first Christmas some 2,000 years ago. According to the Christian calendar, the Christmas season does not *end* on December 25. It *begins* on December 25. It continues for twelve full days, until the evening of January 5, and is followed by Epiphany, which—like Christmas—is both a day and a season.

There also is some overlap between the two Christmases in tradition. Many Christmas customs, such as decorating with holly and ivy, have their origin in ancient pagan winter festivals. In adopting these customs centuries ago, Christians gave them new meaning, and their original meaning was largely forgotten. Non-Christians can keep the same traditions today and never know the meaning that their Christian neighbors attach to these traditions (any more than their Christian neighbors can know the meaning that the customs had hundreds of years ago in very different cultures).

An example: However the Christmas tree originated, millions of families enjoy erecting a tree in their home without ever suspecting that the tree has a specific Christian meaning. For some Christians, it represents the Tree of Life and God's promise of redemption for humanity. But for most people (including most Christians, who aren't aware of the association with the Tree of Life), it's just an evergreen tree that gets put up in the living room because there's no space for it in the dining room, and, anyway, the living room window faces the street, so the neighbors can see it and marvel.

There also is some overlap between the two Christmases in meaning. Even the most dedicated secularist probably will admit that the sense of good will that pervades this time of year can be traced to an angel's proclamation, "Peace on earth, good will to all" (Luke 2:14 paraphrased). Yet these same secularists may deride Luke's story as a childish fantasy and push to forever detach it from any "rational" discussion of peace and good will.

The two Christmases share a large common ground, and this is a cultural battleground. Christmas is a national holiday as well as a religious holy day, so questions of private practice easily become questions of public policy. The debates may be framed as "Put Christ back into Christmas!" or "Keep religion off public property!" Either way, similar arguments have been around for centuries. They go back almost to the origins of Christmas. And they aren't likely to go away in the foreseeable future, because culturally we have so much invested in both Christmases.

LISTEN TO THE MUSIC

If you do not believe that there are two Christmases, listen to the music that you hear on the radio and at stores and shopping malls starting right after Thanksgiving. You will hear two kinds of music. At commercial outlets especially, you will hear mostly songs celebrating winter and the season called Christmas. At other outlets, you also may hear the sacred hymns, carols and songs celebrating the Nativity of Jesus the Messiah the Son of God. And occasionally you will hear a song that tries to bridge the gap.

I have compiled a list of 129 popular songs of the season. You can make your own list, and it might include some songs I missed. New songs come out each year, and some of them are quite good. However many songs you come up with, I think any list that represents the range of music that is played at Christmastime will follow this breakdown of titles:

Sacred—about half
Secular—about half
Mixed—what's left

Let me show you. Table 1 lists sacred carols, hymns and songs of Christmas (not all of them, surely, but the ones you are most likely to hear).

Table 1. Sacred carols, hymns and songs of Christmas

A Cradle in Bethlehem
Angels From the Realms of Glory
Angels We Have Heard on High
Away in a Manger
Breath of Heaven (Mary's Song)
Bring a Torch, Jeanette Isabella
Come, Thou Long-Expected Jesus
Coventry Carol
Do You Hear What I Hear?
Fum, Fum, Fum

Go Tell It on the Mountain
God Rest Ye Merry, Gentlemen
Good Christian (Men) Friends, Rejoice
Hail to the Lord's Anointed
Handel's Hallelujah Chorus
Hark the Herald Angels Sing
In the Bleak Midwinter
Infant Holy, Infant Lowly
I Saw Three Ships
It All Began in Bethlehem
It Came Upon the Midnight Clear
I Wonder as I Wander
Jesu, Joy of Man's Desiring
Jesus Holy, Born So Lowly
Joy to the World
Lo How a Rose E'er Blooming
Love Came Down at Christmas
March of the Kings
Mary, Did You Know
Mary Had a Baby
Mary's Boy Child
O Come, All Ye Faithful
O Come, O Come, Emmanuel
O Holy Night
O Little Town of Bethlehem
O Sing a Song of Bethlehem
Once in Royal David's City
Pat-a-pan
People, Look East
Rise Up, Shepherd, and Follow
See Him Lying in a Bed of Straw
Silent Night
Sing We Now of Christmas

Some Children See Him (James Taylor)
Still, Still, Still
That Boy–Child of Mary
The First Noel
The Friendly Beasts
The Holly and the Ivy
The Little Drummer Boy
The Twelve Days of Christmas
The Virgin Mary Had a Baby Boy
There's a New Kid in Town
There's a Song in the Air
To a Maid Engaged to Joseph
We Three Kings
What Child Is This?
While By My Sheep
While Shepherds Watched Their Flocks
Who Comes This Night? (James Taylor)

Table 2 lists songs that are inherently secular or simply celebrate winter. Again, these aren't all of them, just the ones you are most likely to hear.

Table 2. Secular/winter Christmas songs

(I'm Getting) Nothin' for Christmas
A Candle in the Window
A Christmas Letter
A Christmas to Remember
A Holly Jolly Christmas
All I Want for Christmas Is My Two Front Teeth
All I Want for Christmas Is You
Auld Lang Syne
Baby, It's Cold Outside
Blue Christmas
Boar's Head Carol

Carol of the Bells (Ding Dong Ding)
Christmas Don't Be Late (The Chipmunks Song)
Christmas in Dixie
Christmas in Kilarney
Christmas Is
Christmas Memories
Christmas Time Is Here
Christmas Without You
Deck the Halls
Ding Dong Merrily on High
Don't They Know It's Christmas?
Feliz Navidad
Frosty the Snowman
Grandma Got Run Over by a Reindeer
Happy Holiday
Have Yourself a Merry Little Christmas
Here Comes Santa Claus
Hey, Santa
Home for the Holidays
I Saw Mama Kissing Santa Claus
I'll Be Home for Christmas
It's Beginning to Look a Lot Like Christmas
It's the Most Wonderful Time of the Year
Jingle Bell Rock
Jingle Bells
Jolly Old Saint Nicholas
Let It Snow
Little Saint Nick
Mele Kalikimaka
Must Be Santa
Please Come Home for Christmas
Please, Daddy, Don't Get Drunk on Christmas
Rocking Around the Christmas Tree

Rudolph the Red-Nosed Reindeer
Santa Baby
Santa Claus Is Coming to Town
Silver Bells
Sleigh Ride
Tennessee Christmas
The Christmas Song ("Chestnuts roasting on an open fire...")
The Greatest Gift of All (two versions)
Up on the Housetop
Wassail Song (Here We Come a Wassailing)
We Need a Little Christmas
We Wish You a Merry Christmas
What Christmas Means to Me
White Christmas
Winter Wonderland
Wonderful Christmastime

Table 3 lists songs that mix elements of the sacred and the secular or consciously try to bridge the gap.

Table 3. Carols and songs that mix sacred and secular

All Because of a Baby Boy
A Star Is Born Tonight
Caroling, Caroling
Christmas Is Coming
For Christ's Sake, It's Christmas
Good King Wenceslas
I Heard the Bells on Christmas Day
Joseph and Mary's Boy
O Tannenbaum (O Christmas Tree)

For the record, 60 of the 129 songs (46.5 percent) are sacred, 60 (46.5 percent) are secular and 9 (7 percent) are mixed. These percentages reveal the cultural split over Christmas. It's not that singing "Away in the Manger" is good but singing "Winter Wonderland" is bad. It's just that "Winter Wonderland" has nothing to do with Jesus. It doesn't mention Jesus. Not even once. If all you ever heard were songs like "Winter Wonderland," you might never know that Christmas is about more than winter fun, gifts and that vague sense of good will that everyone feels this time of year because—well, because that's just the way people *feel* this time of year.

Some radio stations play Christmas music nonstop from the day after Thanksgiving until midnight on Christmas Day, and mostly they play the secular songs of Christmas—over and over, ad nauseum. If I hear José Feliciano sing "I wanna wish you a Merry Christmas" one more time, I think I'm gonna gag. I was once trapped in a dentist's chair for more than an hour while secular Christmas music played relentlessly in the background, and I'm not kidding when I say that the music was harder to endure than the root canal.

Now if my count is correct and there are, in fact, about the same number of sacred Christmas songs as there are secular Christmas songs, why do the secular ones get more air time on most radio stations? Some Christians may howl that this is just another sign that Christ is being taken out of Christmas. What it is, indisputably, is a sign that radio stations play to their listening audience, and most of their listeners want to hear the secular songs most of the time. If their listeners wanted to hear sacred songs most of the time, you can be certain that the stations would play them. And guess what? On radio stations devoted to Christian programming, sacred songs *do* get most of the airtime.

HAPPY HOLIDAY(S)

People are so sensitive these days that you risk offending someone simply by saying, "Good morning." So it's natural that there's a lot of verbal sparring over the proper greeting during, you know, that season that follows Thanksgiving. Do you say, "Merry Christmas," or do you say, "Happy Holidays"? You might think this is a small matter, but many people get seriously bent out of shape when they hear the wrong greeting at the deli or the shopping mall.

If you say "Happy Holidays" to someone who wants to hear "Merry Christmas," you're likely to get an earful about how Christ is being driven out of Christmas, yada yada yada. But if you say "Merry Christmas" to someone who wants to hear "Happy Holidays," you're likely to hear about how all mention of Christmas should be banned from the public square, yada yada yada.

Not many years ago, a few merchants instructed their employees to wish customers "Happy Holidays" rather than "Merry Christmas." It's because atheists and other firm non-believers don't want to be told to have a merry something they don't believe in. You just can't tell by looking at someone whether he or she is an atheist or a whatever, so it's safer to say "Happy Holidays." If a guy comes into your checkout lane wearing a turban, you might surmise that he's Sikh and not interested in being wished a "Merry Christmas." Same if a woman appears covered in a Muslim burkha. Otherwise, you're on dangerous ground wishing anybody much of anything beyond the generic "Happy Holidays." Retailers often go way out of their way to avoid offending people, so naturally they're going to be very careful here. That earns them no slack from some Christians and political pundits who see vast conspiracies to destroy their way of life.

If you go into a book and gift shop or other establishment that announces itself as Christian, you certainly should expect to hear "Merry Christmas." And no matter how you are greeted, there's nothing preventing *you* from responding with a hearty, "Merry Christmas!" But if you encounter someone you don't know in the public square, why should you either expect or demand that the person say "Merry Christmas"? What right do you have to force your cultural tradition on someone else? Why are you so offended that others don't believe exactly the same way you do? Why does this *threaten* you so much?

Some Christians, knowing that the man in a turban is Sikh and the woman in the burkha is Muslim, may actually go out of their way to wish them a merry Christmas. They will imagine that they are witnessing to their beliefs rather than merely being boorishly disrespectful of the beliefs of others. Don't bother asking these people how they would feel if someone wished them a "Happy Hannukah!" or a "Happy Kwanzaa!" They will not understand if you accuse them of operating out of an imperialistic paradigm. Rather, they will accuse *you* of being imperialistic because *you* are trying to stamp out *their* right of free speech. Rights, in their view, go only one way. And *they* got 'em. Others don't.

You'll get a similar response from dedicated secularists. They'll go ballistic when you wish them anything beyond a "good day." And be careful of "Goodbye!" It is, after all, a shortened form of "God be with you!"

"Happy Holidays" covers multiple occasions—Thanksgiving, Christmas, Hanukkah, Kwanzaa, New Year's. It's a simple expression of good will to someone you don't know, and it's more personal than generics such as, "Have a nice day." But it sounds like we're going to have to fight over this thing for awhile because fighting over it is so much easier than acknowledging the truth it represents. The truth of it is that there are two Christmases, one cultural and one religious, and as much as they are alike, they are as different as night and day, and we are not likely to bridge the gap between them. Our ongoing culture wars will not allow it.

WHO STOLE CHRISTMAS?

Thanks to Dr. Seuss, we know that the Grinch stole Christmas. He stole it from the Whos of Whoville. But he had a change of heart and returned it.

Now we hear that some others have gotten into the act. Political right-wingers say there's a "liberal plot" to steal Christmas. Not so, lefties reply, because the self-appointed "cultural warriors" of the right have already stolen it.

The original theft of Christmas is many centuries old, some historians contend. It was the Christians who first stole Christmas. They stole it from the pagans. (Actually, as we'll see, it's more likely that the pagans stole the date from Christians.)

Just about everybody appears convinced that somebody stole, or is stealing, or is plotting to steal Christmas from somebody else, and something ought to be done about it. But what? Until and unless we as a society can agree on who stole/is stealing/is plotting to steal what from whom, it's hard to know what to do to stop it, if it isn't already too late to stop it, if we're sure we even *want* to stop it. I mean, maybe we ought to just let them *have* it, if they want it so badly.

The Grinch gave the Whos their Christmas back because he didn't want the gifts and goodies for himself. He stole them only to keep the Whos from enjoying them. What are the motives of today's Christmas thieves?

Some say there is a war *on* Christmas. I think it's more accurate to say that there is a war *over* Christmas. Even more accurately, there is a war over *culture*, and extremists on both sides hope to use Christmas as a club to beat the other side into submission.

TWO CHRISTMASES, FOUR CHOICES

You can have a "Holly Jolly Christmas," or you can have a "Joy to the World" Christmas, or you can have both, or neither. Here's a glance at that relatively slim spectrum of possibilities:

- You can have a "Holly Jolly Christmas" with decorations and parties and gifts and Santa and lots of fun and good will to all. Jesus? Who's he?

This is the secular Christmas enjoyed by many millions of people around the world. (In Japan, where only a tiny percentage of the people are Christian, Christmas is hugely popular.) This is the cultural Christmas that so often leaves people exhausted by all the activity but yearning for something they missed. Basically, it's just another holiday—like Halloween, only bigger. Who cares how it got started as long as it's fun?

- You can have a "Joy to the World" Christmas with songs and prayers, and it's all focused on what God is doing for humanity in Jesus. But even if you stage a "Birthday Party for Jesus" with cake and punch, the celebration is pretty spare compared with what the rest of the world is doing.

This is the sacred Christmas that many Christians *say* they want. They experience it mainly in church and usually don't try very hard to reproduce it at home—especially on Christmas Day, when they are probably enjoying a thoroughly secular family holiday.

- You can have both a "Holly Jolly Christmas" and a "Joy to the World" Christmas by enjoying the best of both worlds.

This is the alternative that most Christians pursue today. If you've tried this, you know that living in two worlds can just about drive you crazy. The typical complaint is that the "Holly Jolly Christmas" so overshadows the "Joy to the World" Christmas that you lose sight of Jesus in all the holiday madness. Getting sidetracked certainly is easy enough to do. Asking "Where's Jesus in all this?" is what started me thinking about this book. But isn't "Where's Jesus?" a question that Christians need to ask on *all* occasions? Aren't Christians *called* to live in two worlds? Aren't we supposed to live with one foot in heaven and the other on earth, at least until God brings heaven down to earth, as is promised in the book of Revelation? If we can't get this balancing act right at Christmas, how can we hope to get it right with other, even more complex, issues?

- You can have neither a "Holly Jolly Christmas" nor a "Joy to the World" Christmas. You can just do without Christmas altogether.

Maybe, if you live in a cave or something, you can pull this off without much effort. As much as you try to ignore Christmas, it's not going to go away. The crowds won't disperse when you go to the mall on an errand. The music and the decorations will be constant reminders of what is on everyone else's mind. But if you've ever gone through a Super Bowl season or a March Madness without a favorite team in the competition, you know how irrelevant those games can be to you. You can make *Christmas* irrelevant, too, if you try hard enough and focus on other things.

Focus on what's important to you and ignore the rest. Maybe *that's* the secret to making Christmas work for you, however you choose to celebrate or not celebrate the season. But now we're exploring rough terrain. Now we're talking about the power, and the limits, of individual responsibility. It's much more enjoyable to complain about the guy down the street whose gaudy Christmas lights make his driveway look like an airport runway.

ANTI-CHRISTMAS RANTS

Partly because of its dual nature, the Christmas season is a bundle of contradictions. Christmas is a religious holy day. It also is a family–oriented holiday. Christmas is a spiritual season. It also is a commercial season. Christmas is a time of revelry and abandon. It also is a time of intense longing and loneliness. Christmas is a time of peace and good will to all. It also is a time of political posturing and partisan bickering. Christmas is a time of giving and sharing. It also is a time of gluttony and hoarding.

Christmas is a collection of huge expectations and heartbreaking disappointments. No wonder people love to gripe about it and try to use it to their own advantage.

The anti–Christmas rant is a tradition that goes back to the early centuries of Christianity. These tirades can be entertaining, but only some of them are enlightening. In the true department are these:

- "Christmas is an economic juggernaut."

Keeping Christmas

The American economy is structured around Christmas. TV weather forecasters may chatter endlessly about hopes for a white Christmas, but retailers are dreaming of a *black* Christmas.[1] In a typical year, they will make one-quarter of their yearly sales and perhaps 60 percent of their profits between Thanksgiving and Christmas. The day after Thanksgiving is called Black Friday because sales that day are said to push many businesses out of the red and into the black for the year, so Christmas sales represent profit. "This is our harvest time," F.W. Woolworth told his store managers in 1891.[2]

How big is the harvest? In 2018, holiday retail sales set a record of $707.5 billion. In the previous 18 years, sales increased by at least 2.1 percent each year, except for the recession years of 2008 and 2009, when sales actually dropped from the year before.[3]

- "Christmas topples forests."

The National Christmas Tree Association estimates that 25 million to 30 million trees are sold each year.[4] If they were grown at the recommended rate of 1,000 trees per acre, that translates to a minimum of 250,000 acres, or 390 square miles. That's bigger than all five boroughs of New York City. You know what else is similar in size? The Dead Sea. Astronauts say they can easily see the Dead Sea from outer space. So each year, Christmas tree harvests denude an area of land you could see from space. (Happily, it does not all occur in one place, so you *can't* actually see it from space.)

- "Christmas taxes our social systems."

For the U.S. Postal Service, 2007 was a record year. It delivered 20 billion pieces of mail between Thanksgiving and Christmas. Volume has fallen sharply from that level, to 16 billion pieces annually.[5] But if you want an earful, ask some postal workers what they think of the Christmas rush. A lot of that mail and other Christmas debris ends up in the trash, so it shouldn't be surprising that trash pickup around the holidays is 25 percent larger than normal.[6]

Police and other public safety officers who have to work on Christmas Eve yearn for a silent night but rarely get it. Mental health professionals have many Christmas-related problems to deal with, including the anxiety many people feel when they start getting credit card bills for their Christmas spending.

- "Christmas fails its social purpose."

Two Christmases

In a memorable outburst in *The New Republic* titled "Why I Hate Christmas," economist James S. Henry observed: "The holiday is an insidious and overlooked factor in America's dwindling savings rates, slack work ethic, and high crime rates. Nor does Christmas truly fulfill its purposed distributional objective: the transfer of gifts to those who need them." [7] Similar sentiments have been expressed by the likes of economist Joel Waldfogel and national columnist George F. Will.[8]

As theologian Miroslav Volf explains, it's as if the Wise Men journeyed to Bethlehem to pay homage to the newborn King and, rather than giving presents to the Babe in the Manger, they exchanged gifts among themselves.[9]

Or again, from ecologist and social critic Bill McKibben: "We celebrate the birth of One who told us to give everything to the poor by giving each other motorized tie racks."[10]

Those are among the true—or, at least, mostly true—rants about Christmas. Alas, Christmas rants also are responsible for several major misconceptions about Christmas.

- "Christmas is a pagan holiday."

Surprisingly, you hear this line from both Christian and secular critics of the season. Both use it to discredit the very notion of celebrating the birth of Jesus in December.

According to the Christian critics, there is nothing Christian about Christmas. The Bible does not tell us to celebrate Jesus' birth, so we have no business doing it. The whole idea is pagan nonsense, and we ought not to corrupt our pure faith with this kind of thing.

According to the secular critics, Christians stole a winter festival from the pagans and pasted the Christian story on top of it. The date, the customs, just about everything that makes Christmas the fun season it is—it all came from the pagans. What hypocrites Christians are that they won't even acknowledge their theft!

Here is the unvarnished truth, which we will explore later in more detail: The earliest Christians did not celebrate the birth of Jesus. When they decided that they wanted to celebrate the event, they were uncertain when to do it. For reasons that are somewhat obscure (and, of course, fiercely debated), they chose a date that fell during a time of winter merrymaking. Many of the customs of this merrymaking "rubbed off" on the celebration of Jesus' birth.

So it is true that many Christmas traditions have pagan influences. But it is *not* true that Christmas is a pagan holiday with a Christian veneer. *That* story was the invention of seventeenth-century English Puritans, who campaigned against Christmas so vigorously that they almost destroyed it. Neither Christian nor secular critics of Christmas honor the truth when they perpetuate the "pagan Christmas" lie.

- "Christmas is not in the Bible, so we shouldn't celebrate it."

True, the New Testament nowhere tells us to celebrate the day of Jesus' birth. (Nor does it tell us *not* to celebrate. Nor does it tell us to celebrate the Resurrection of Jesus at Easter.) The "can't find it commanded in the Bible" thing is what academics politely call an "argument from silence," and most such arguments are thoroughly bogus. You can use the same argument to contend that churches should not have indoor plumbing, air conditioning, computers or coffeepots. This line of argument (it can't really be called a line of *reasoning*) may honor that dark part of you that wants to control the lives of others, but it does not honor God. So just drop it, OK?

- "Christmas is about gluttony and excess."

Even if you're trying to eat right, it's hard to control your diet when you are constantly exposed to rich foods and sugar-saturated cookies and candy. But, as we'll see, there are good historical reasons for such excess in early winter. And always remember, no one is *forcing* you to overeat. That's *your* decision and no one else's. *Your* Christmas can be different.

- "Christmas is about commerce and greed."

Yes, our economy hinges on overspending at Christmas. But nobody *forces* you to overspend. Why *do* Americans, who so pride themselves on their "rugged individualism," run like lemmings to shopping centers to buy the same "hot gift items" that everybody else wants? Just because the "Bankrupt Me, Elmo" doll tops the gift charts does not mean that you or anyone you know actually *needs* one. So why are you shivering in line at 5 a.m. on Black Friday waiting for the toy store to open?

- "The expectations surrounding Christmas are just too high."

Christmas is supposed to be a season of joy, but many people suffer depression instead because their expectations can never be met. The Percy Faith song "Christmas Is" drips with saccharine sentiment and promotes the fantasy that Christmas is "when all your wishes come true." What a cruel lie! We might wish it were so, but it clearly is not. We can't all get home for Christmas, and all our loved ones can't be near. Santa will disappoint some children and miss others altogether. That brightly wrapped gift box may contain something that delights you beyond expectation—or just another useless doodad to toss in a closet with all the others.

- "The emotional toll is just too high."

Anyone who's lost a loved one to death late in the year will find the first Thanksgiving and Christmas without that loved one sadly different from any before. That melancholy may linger to later Thanksgivings and Christmases as well. To them, the sounds of carols and sleigh bells may be like the sounds of July 4 fireworks to military veterans suffering from PTSD. Theirs may always be a "Blue Christmas." No matter how many "Blue Christmas" worship services they attend, they'll always find their emotions triggered by the winter holidays.

If you know someone whose winter days are especially dark because of a loss, please go out of your way to support them during the season. And remember that it's not the fault of the holiday that they suffer. They suffer because of a great loss, and what they lost was a cherished relationship that was made happier by the holiday that persists even though their loved one is gone.

- "Christmas is too sentimental."

One reason we try so hard to celebrate Christmas "right" is that we want to recapture a magical memory of that "perfect" Christmas. Probably it never happened, or at least never happened the way we remember it, but we *want* it to happen. So we try to "re-create" it. Today's cultural Christmas is basically the creation of those who lived during the reign of Britain's Queen Victoria in the second half of the nineteenth century. They imagined that they were restoring Christmas to its past glory, but in fact they were creating Christmas anew in their own optimistic and progressive image. We always create Christmas anew, even as we try to make today's Christmas the Christmas that never was. And when our time together is at an end and our loved ones are piling into their cars to go home, don't we get tight-throated and misty-eyed? Surely there is nothing wrong with *that* kind of sentimentality.

- "The lights and tinsel blind us to the real meaning of Christmas."

Yes, it happens so easily. As poet W.H. Auden writes in *For the Time Being*, "Well, so that is that … Once again as in previous years we have seen the actual vision and failed to do more than entertain it as an agreeable possibility."[11] And yet some people never appear blinded by the holiday glare. What's their secret? Are they all candidates for sainthood? Or have they simply discovered that centering their lives on Jesus helps them turn back many temptations?

- "Christmas is religious. It belongs behind closed doors, not in the public square."

A few Christians make this case, but its champions are mostly secularists. Some secularists are out to keep Baby in the Manger scenes and the like off of public property. Others want the public schools purged of all winter frivolity, even if does not point to Jesus. In other words, some want the sacred Christmas banned; others want the secular Christmas banned as well.

It is hard to understand what sort of "public square" these people envision. Apparently it is one that is ignorant of history and devoid of any cultural influence except that approved and mandated by the ruling majority (or ruling minority). And how exactly would this be any different from the "theocracy" that many of these same secularists say they dread so much?

WHEN STATUES LAUGH

In the pages that follow, we will look more closely at these issues and others, talk about how we got to these places and explore some paths to *better* places. Before we go there, let me tell you a story that I think encapsulates the contradictory approaches to such issues and suggests how intractable people are in their attitudes and how hard it will be even to start a dialogue about what the problem is.

Several years ago, the Kansas City Zoo received a complaint from a man who identified himself as Christian.[12] It seems that the man was walking with his family down the Tiger Trail, and he was shocked—*shocked!*—to see two statues of the Buddha beside the trail. Not only that, people were honoring this offensive "idol" by rubbing its head and belly. Christians, of course, are not allowed to display crosses or Nativity scenes on public property. It's an obvious case of religious discrimination!

Or is it less a case of discrimination and more a case of ignorance and confusion?

- A Buddhist leader in Kansas City was quick to point out that the statues were not of the Buddha but of Ho Tai, whom he described as the patron saint of children, sort of like a Buddhist Santa Claus.

- *The* Buddha is Siddhartha Gautama, or Gautama Buddha, the founder of Buddhism. He lived in India several centuries before the time of Jesus. "Buddha" means "enlightened one." Gautama Buddha is revered as an enlightened human being, but he is not worshipped as a god, nor do Buddhists pray to him. (And some Buddhists worship no god at all.)

- Ho Tai is a Buddhist monk who lived in China more than a thousand years after the Buddha. Because he also attained enlightenment, Ho Tai also is called Buddha. Sometimes he is called "the laughing Buddha" because statues of him show him as jolly, where Gautama Buddha is most often portrayed as serene. Ho Tai is almost always fat, too, where Gautama Buddha is only sometimes fat.

- In Kansas City, people also rub the head and nose of a bronze boar that sits in a little fountain on a public walkway in the Country Club Plaza. In Springfield, Illinois, capital of the Land of Lincoln, people rub the prominent nose of a bronze bust of Abraham Lincoln. In an apartment house I know, people rub the brass ball that tops a stair railing. Rubbing these things makes them shine. It's not exactly an act of worship.

- The Buddha statues were placed beside the Tiger Trail, along with some concrete pagodas and other statuary, to evoke a sense of place. Buddhists live all around the world, but they are concentrated in some of the same places that tigers live. Tell me, what sense of place is evoked by a cross or by a Nativity scene? What would a cross beside the trail tell you about the land of tigers?

If offended Christians in Kansas City raised enough of a stink, they might have gotten the laughing Buddha statues removed. Similar complaints might lead to the removal of other cultural icons as well. Soon the zoo could be devoid of all human meaning. It would be a sterile place where exotic animals are kept in cages for the amusement of creatures that are allegedly superior to the animals in some way, although they cannot even disagree agreeably about the most basic of things.

This also may be the future of the public arena in America. The irony is that it won't get this way solely because of complaints from atheists and other secularists. It also will be because of complaints from Christians, who can be just as intolerant of others as others are of them.

The irony goes deeper. There are two Christmases today. It is likely that, to one extent or another, there always *were* two Christmases. But one reason the secular Christmas is bigger today is that Christian intolerance pretty much stamped out the sacred Christmas in some places a few centuries ago. Yes, there was once a war *on* Christmas, and it wasn't waged by wild-eyed Bible-burning secularists. It was waged by *Christians*. We'll come to that story soon, right after we look at the origins of Christmas—and the war that still rages over who stole what from whom.

Chapter Two

Why December 25?

Ebenezer Scrooge's nephew, Fred, was right. Christmas is a "good time—a kind, forgiving, charitable, pleasant time: the only time I know of, in the long calendar of the year, when men and women seem by one consent to open their shut–up hearts freely . . ."

But Scrooge was right, too. So much about Christmas is pure humbug.

The problem is that Christmas carries too much baggage. The season celebrates not only the birth of Jesus but also jingle bells, Frosty the Snowman, chestnuts roasting on an open fire, you'd better watch out 'cause Santa Claus is coming to town, I'll be home for the holidays (if only in my dreams) and best wishes for a prosperous and happy new year.

Wasn't there a time, you may wonder, when Christmas was simple? Wasn't there a time when revelry and gift–giving weren't so much a part of the season? Wasn't there a time when there was only one Christmas, not the two we have now? Wasn't there a time when Christmas was focused entirely on Jesus?

The answer is no. At least, probably not—and if so, not for long. That's one of the reasons Christmas is such a mess today. It's been a mess from the start.

The short version of the story is that early Christians chose to celebrate the birth of Jesus during a season of winter merrymaking. Some of the merrymaking "rubbed off" on the birthday party. The result is a celebration that has always been as much secular holiday as it is religious holy day. In the public arena called Christmas, the secular and the sacred regularly slug it out.

We may pout about how terrible this situation is. Or we may consider it more a reflection of what the Incarnation of God in Jesus is all about. When God enters our world, what happens is not always neat and pretty, but it can have great redemptive value.

THE BIRTH OF JESUS

The earliest Christians did not celebrate the birth of Jesus. Birthdays just weren't important to the struggling faith. New theologies were emerging that had to be embraced or denounced—and if heresies were not troublesome enough, there always was the periodic threat of persecution by the authorities. Birthdays also were considered to be a pagan affectation. The date of a saint's martyrdom was more likely to be remembered than the date of his or her birth, just as the death and resurrection of Jesus were remembered at Easter. The date of your death was your true birth, your entrance into eternal life beyond this vale of tears.

Only "the worthless man" loved things connected to birthdays. That was the opinion of the church leader Origen of Alexandria, who lived from about 185 to 254 CE. Origen noted that Scripture contains no record of a birthday being observed by a righteous person. No, the only mentions of birthdays in the Bible are the Egyptian pharaoh, who on his birthday hanged his chief baker, and the despotic ruler Herod Antipas, who on his birthday beheaded John the Baptizer.[13] Oh, and there is poor Job, who did not celebrate but rather cursed the day he was born. (Job 3:1–26)

There also was the question of *when* to celebrate the occasion. If anyone in the church ever knew on what date Jesus was born, we have no record of it. The gospels of Mark and John say nothing of Jesus' birth, and the birth narratives in Matthew and Luke don't mention the year, let alone the month and day. The writers of the gospels were more interested in the significance of the event than its date.

Yet even before Origen's fulminations against the propriety of birthdays, scholars were busy advancing educated guesses. It was in the spring or summer, some suggested, because that's when shepherds most likely would be keeping watch in the fields at night, as Luke 2:8 says they were. It definitely was not in December, these sages said, because that's in Israel's wet season, when animals would be kept sheltered after dark. No, others said, certain sheep were always kept outdoors, whatever the season. Those were the sheep destined for sacrifice in the Temple at Jerusalem. What could be more appropriate than the herders of these sheep being the first to hear of the birth of one whose sacrifice will save the world?[14]

If the date of Jesus' birth is so uncertain, you may wonder how we wound up celebrating the event in December, and specifically December 25. The explanation is more elusive than we would like. It would help if we had some record from an ecumenical council, or a notation from the diary of some prominent historical figure: "Created Christmas today—don't know what will come of it." But we have no such documentation. The people who created Christmas didn't record the how or the why or the when of it. Almost everything we think we know is an assumption based on an inference drawn from limited data.

It's not only the essence of Christmas that is disputed. The very *history* of Christmas is disputed. We fight not only about whether and how to celebrate it, but also over when it was created, by whom and for what purpose. The following account is indebted to the great French scholar Louis Duchesne and his modern heirs in the search for the real history of Christmas: Thomas J. Talley, Susan K. Roll, Joseph F. Kelly, William J. Tighe, Oscar Cullman, and Andrew McGowan.

THE BIRTH OF CHRISTMAS

The creation of Christmas came during a turbulent period in the life of the Christian church. For most of its first three hundred years, Christianity was an outlaw religion. Sometimes it was tolerated by the Roman state, sometimes it was severely persecuted. But it not only survived, it thrived. Then, almost overnight, the situation was reversed. Christianity ceased being an enemy of the state and became a function of the state.

The Emperor Constantine had a knack for dramatizing things. He liked to say that he was inspired to accept Christianity by a vision he saw in the sky on the eve of a great military victory. Many historians think that his vision was inspired more by enlightened politics. He realized that the suppression of Christianity was not in the empire's best interests and that Christians would make better allies than enemies. For, remarkably, Christians remained loyal to the empire even when the empire persecuted them. Their major quarrel with the state was over its insistence that the emperor was divine, and their chief crime was failure to worship the emperor. Remove those two impediments and they would be ideal citizens: industrious, trustworthy, stable, and moral.

Whatever his motivation, in 313 CE Constantine took steps to legalize Christianity, and he became its champion. Within seventy years, Christianity became not simply the dominant but the *official* religion of the Roman Empire, the *required* religion of millions. In the span of a lifetime, it went from being the object of persecution to the perpetrator of it.

Those who had been "in the world but not of it" now were charged with running it. The weight of the empire was on their shoulders. And the empire was slowly collapsing. The Greco–Roman world was about to be swept away by barbarian incursions from every quarter. That Christianity survived the collapse tells how well it adapted to its new circumstances. But the changes shook the foundations of the church and profoundly altered its nature.

At the beginning of the fourth century, the Roman church was politically weak and theologically insecure, buffeted by state policies it could not control and heresies it could not eradicate. Its ritual was relatively simple and its organization was loose and mostly decentralized. By the end of the century, the church was rich and powerful and pretty much in control of its theological destiny. It had an elaborate and impressive rite (modeled after Roman court practice) and a firm hierarchy. It had infiltrated every sector of Roman society, every sphere of activity, every circle of thought. It had made itself, as the Apostle Paul once suggested, "all things to all people" so that by all means some might be saved (1 Corinthians 9:22). It had become a truly catholic (which is to say, universal) church, and also one that we today might recognize as *Roman* Catholic. It was ready to inherit the world.

Somewhere in the midst of all this turmoil, people began celebrating Jesus' birth on December 25.

WHO STOLE WHAT FROM WHOM?

The year 336 CE is the earliest we can say with any certainty that the birth of Jesus was commemorated on December 25 in Rome. The evidence comes in a document known as the Philocalian Calendar, or the Chronograph of 354. It's an illustrated almanac and calendar assembled by an artist named Philocalus. Though the document itself dates to 354 CE, parts of the calendar it reproduces go back to 336, and that is where we find the notation that Jesus was born during the reign of Augustus on December 25. The *year* of Jesus' birth is not mentioned, but the entry confidently states that it happened on a Friday.[15]

If some Romans were celebrating the birth of Jesus on December 25 as early as 336, the custom was slow to spread. Fifty years later, in a sermon in 386 in Antioch, Bishop John Chrysostom mentions that "it is not the tenth year since this day has become clearly known to us," though it was "known from of old to the inhabitants of the West."[16] Those remarks seem to date the arrival of the celebration in Antioch about 376. That's only a couple of years before Gregory of Nazianzus introduced it in Constantinople, the Eastern capital of the Roman Empire.[17]

Evidence for a December 25 celebration *before* 336 is slight. A commentary by Hippolytus of Rome (who died about 235 CE) states that Jesus was born on December 25, a Wednesday. But some scholars suspect that a later hand has tampered with this text. A remark by Augustine of Hippo (354–430) could be interpreted to suggest that some Christians observed the December 25 date as early as 311, but it's a stretch.[18] So 336 is the earliest we can push the adoption of December 25 as a date of public celebration. We have to wonder both *why* that date was chosen and *when* it was chosen.

The standard explanation is that Christians stole the date from the pagans. This is the version that you will hear most often, especially in "educated" circles. It is the accepted version that is repeated in many accounts as if it were the undisputed truth.

Christians were looking for a date to celebrate the birth of Jesus. They decided to steal an existing pagan holiday, thus turning the day to their own uses.

What they stole, according to this story, was the *Dies Natalis Solis Invicti*, "the Birthday of the Unconquered Sun." This was a solar festival created by the Emperor Aurelian in 274 CE in an attempt to revive flagging solar religion. It is widely thought that Constantine hoped to bolster solar religion by fusing it with Christianity. Perhaps he pushed the creation of Christmas to accomplish this end.

But there are several huge problems with the notion that Christians stole the Birthday of the Sun and converted it to the Birthday of the Son. First, there is no evidence for this theft. Second, there are strong suggestions that the *pagans* were the ones trying to steal the date from the Christians—and that they succeeded, for a time, before the Christians got it back.

The major piece of evidence for Christians stealing the date turns out to be the presumption that the pagans had the date first. Well, 274 is earlier than 336, so it's obvious, isn't it? Chronology trumps everything.

At least, that is the assumption of the "history of religions" school of history. This school originated in nineteenth-century Germany. Its fundamental supposition is that all religious ideas evolve from other religious ideas. The "history of religions" school takes literally only one statement in the Bible, and that comes from Ecclesiastes 1:9: "What has been is what will be, and what has been done is what will be done; there is nothing new under the sun." Everything has to be derived from something that came earlier. There is no possibility of innovation. There is no possibility that God might declare, as in Isaiah 43:19: "I am about to do a new thing!" This restrictive line of thinking has governed much research and writing about the history of Christmas for 150 years.

But what if the "history of religions" people got the cart and the horse confused? What if Aurelian decided to declare December 25 the Birthday of the Sun to counter Christian insistence that it was the Birthday of the Son? What if Christians actually *believed* that Jesus was born on December 25—and had believed it for a long time before Aurelian tried to steal the day from them?

The earliest historical reference we have to Christians celebrating the birth of Jesus on December 25 is the Philocalian Calendar. The earliest historical reference we have to Romans celebrating the Birthday of the Sun on December 25 is . . . the Philocalian Calendar.[19]

The truth is, we can't prove *who* got to the date first. But we *can* show that Christians thought they had good reason to think that Jesus was born on December 25. We are going detour now into some "alternative histories" that may be more accurate than the history so many people have accepted without question for so long.

ALTERNATIVE HISTORIES, PART 1

Nobody knew on what date Jesus was born, but that didn't stop them from speculating. Even while Origen of Alexandria was railing against the idea of celebrating birthdays, other church fathers were trying to compute Jesus' birthday. Clement of Alexandria (who lived about the same time as Origen, from about 150 to 215 CE) heard reports of several dates in the spring, including April 20, April 21 and May 20.[20] However, Clement preferred a winter date: January 6. (Remember that date. It's important.)

Nobody knew on what date Jesus was born. But some people thought they knew on what date Jesus *died*. And for them, knowing when he died was just as good, because everybody knew that great men always died on their *birthday*.

The concept is called "integral age" or "whole age." It's hard for most of us to swallow these days, but it made perfect sense to certain ancient sages. The idea is that Scripture cannot be wrong. Not only is Scripture right, it is *exactly* right. So when Deuteronomy 34:7 says, "Moses was 120 years old when he died," that means that Moses did not die at the age of 119 years and eleven months or at the age of 120 years and four months or any other odd combination of days, weeks, months, and years. No, if Scripture says that Moses died at the age of 120, that's *exactly* how old he was. He was 120 years old, plus or minus *zero* days.

The only way for that to happen, of course, is if he died on his birthday.

Great men thus lived whole or complete lives. The date of a patriarch or a prophet's death was the same date that his mother bore him and the same date that he was born into new life in Paradise. (It was probably just as well that few people in those days knew their birth dates. Who wants to know the date on which you are going to die?)

Notice that this theory does not actually establish what we today would consider a credible argument for the date for someone's birth. But it does establish why people could *believe* that a certain date was someone's birthday.

If we follow this theory, we can calculate Jesus' birthday from the day of his death. The gospels tell us that it was during the Passover, a Jewish festival whose date is determined by a lunar calendar. The gospel of John says it was the day lambs were sacrificed, the 14th day of the month of Nisan. From at least 200 CE, some scholars calculated that in the year that Jesus died, 14 Nisan fell on March 25 on the Julian calendar. (Actually, it appears that this calculation is wrong. But whether the date is historically accurate or not is irrelevant. Such authorities as Hippolytus of Rome and Tertullian of Carthage *thought* it was accurate. Based on what they considered to be scientific calculations, they thought the historic date of Jesus' death was March 25.)

So we arrive at a date of March 25 for both the death and the birth of Jesus. OK, it's a long way from March 25 to December 25, isn't it? Nine months, in fact. If you are a theologian who is trying to calculate the date of Jesus' birth from the date of his death, you have to ask yourself an important question. Which has theological priority: the date on which the God–man Jesus is *born*, or the date on which God is *incarnated* in human flesh, the date that Jesus is *conceived* in the womb of the Virgin Mary? Certainly, the incarnation is more important because that's when God actually assumes human form. So what happens on March 25 is not the *birth* of Jesus but the *incarnation and conception* of Jesus. That pushes the *birth* nine months later ... to December 25.

That's what Sextus Julius Africanus concluded in 221 CE.

Relatively little is known about Julius, but he was the first Christian to be recognized as a real historian, and his work was highly influential. He was born in north Africa about 160 CE and died around 240. He is sometimes called a bishop, but it's not certain he was even a priest. He was well educated, however, and he is credited with several works of literature, including a five-volume *Chronicle* of world events that was the standard history of the world for hundreds of years.

Julius begins his story on the first day of creation, which he asserts was a March 25 exactly 5,500 years before the incarnation of Jesus. Why March 25? Because, according to the Julian calendar, March 25 is the spring equinox, the first day of spring, that season when it appears that the whole world is being re-created. On what more perfect day could creation have occurred?

According to Julius, God began a new creation on the same day that God began the first creation. God became incarnate in human flesh on March 25 and Jesus was born nine months later on December 25.

Note the well-documented date of this writing. This is 221 CE, which is 53 years *before* 274 CE, when the Emperor Aurelian will start a festival on a date that Christians are alleged to have stolen from him.

Still, the claim for December 25 as Jesus' birthday was far from settled. Another key document of the same era as Julius followed similar logic to a *different* conclusion. *De Pascha Computus*, or *Computing the Date of Easter*, is an anonymous tract that dates to 243 CE. It agrees that the first day of creation was the vernal equinox, or March 25 on the Julian calendar. Genesis 1:4 says that on the first day of creation, God created light and "God separated the light from the darkness." Surely God separated them *equally*, so the first day of creation must have been a day when light and darkness were equal. That is, it must have been an equinox day. There are two candidates: spring and fall. The spring equinox wins because spring is the season of creation.

But now comes a twist. Although God creates light on the first day of creation, it's not until the *fourth* day that God creates the earth's main source of light, the sun. For Christians, Jesus is "the sun of righteousness" referred to in Malachi 4:2. Therefore, *De Pascha* says, Jesus must have been born on the fourth day of creation, or March 28.

Like so many other dates proposed for Jesus' birth, March 28 did not stick. But the March 25–December 25 relationship that Julius proposed had more holding power. Shortly after 400 CE, Augustine of Hippo wrote his magnus opus *On the Trinity*. He reported that Jesus "is believed to have been conceived on the 25th of March, upon which day also he suffered," and he was born, "according to tradition," on December 25.[21] What Augustine doesn't say is that in creating this tradition, some scholars followed different trails than that blazed by Julius and still arrived at the same destination.

ALTERNATIVE HISTORIES, PART 2

De solstitiis et aequinoctiis, or *On Solstices and Equinoxes*, is a document from north Africa that dates to the late 300s. It accepts March 25 as the date on which Jesus was both conceived and died and December 25 as the date of his birth. It also advances an interesting argument from Scripture for December 25 being his birthday.

The early chapters of the gospel of Luke tell about the births of Jesus of his kinsman John (who in adulthood will be called John the Baptizer and will be beheaded on Herod Antipas's birthday). John's father, Zechariah, belongs to the priestly order of Abijah and serves in the Temple in Jerusalem twice a year. John's mother, Elizabeth, also comes from a priestly family. After telling of Elizabeth's pregnancy, Luke says that "in the sixth month," an angel appears to Mary to tell her that she also will become pregnant. If you assume that Luke means the "sixth month" of Elizabeth's pregnancy, you can conclude that John is six months older than Jesus. So you can calculate the date of Jesus' birth if you can figure out when John was born.

Happily, Luke says that Zechariah completes his service in the Temple shortly before Elizabeth conceives. Search rabbinical records for the calendars governing such things and, sure enough, you can calculate Zechariah's dates of service and plausibly propose a date for John's conception in late September.

Now comes a huge leap of logic, or faith, or both. You can conclude that John was conceived on September 23 and born on June 24, meaning that Jesus was conceived on March 25 and born on December 25. According to the Julian calendar, those dates are the four cardinal points of the year.

Here's how it works:

- John is conceived at the autumnal equinox and born at the summer solstice.
- Jesus is conceived at the spring equinox and born at the winter solstice.
- Jesus dies on the same date as his conception, the spring equinox.
- John dies on the same date as his birth, the summer solstice.

Here's an illustration that shows it.

Table 4. Solstices and equinoxes

	June 24 Summer solstice John born & dies	
March 25 Spring equinox Jesus conceived & dies	Ol' Sol	September 25 Autumnal equinox John conceived
	December 25 Winter solstice Jesus born	

It is appropriate that John is born and dies at the summer solstice, because after that date days start getting shorter and the nights start getting longer. John once said of his relationship with Jesus: "He must increase, but I must decrease" (John 3:30). The time of John is passing. You can see it in the shortening of the days. Soon the world will witness the glory of the Son, dawning from the darkest of days at the winter equinox.

To us today, the whole scheme may seem contrived and artificial, but to the anonymous author(s) of *De solstitiis*, it made perfect sense that these events should fit so neatly into the calendar year. It's all part of God's glorious plan for saving humanity!

The argument from John's birthday was not limited to *De solstitiis* in north Africa. At roughly the same time that *De solstitiis* was being written, far to the east in Antioch, John Chrysostom was telling a similar story to urge his churches to celebrate the birth of Jesus on December 25. Chrysostom argued that December 25 was the historic date of the Nativity, so that's when it should be celebrated. But his churches apparently heard him reluctantly. In Antioch, they had been accustomed to celebrating Jesus' birth on January 6.

Yes, there were *two* Christmases even way back then.

EAST IS EAST AND WEST IS WEST

At the request of Russian Orthodox Christians, the world-renowned Christmas tree in Rockefeller Center in New York stays lighted every year until January 7, when the Russian Orthodox celebrate Christmas. That is, it's January 7 according to the Gregorian calendar that most of the world follows. It's December 25 according to the Julian calendar that the Russian Orthodox Church follows. The dates are different because the Julian calendar leaks time. It loses 11 minutes every year, or an entire day every 143 years. (Among other things, that means that even though the Julian calendar lists December 25 as the winter solstice, it hasn't really been the winter solstice for 2,000 years.)

Most Orthodox Christians accept a revised Julian calendar that keeps pace with the Gregorian calendar, but the Russian Orthodox and Jerusalem Orthodox stick to the old Julian calendar. Their December 25 is January 7 for just about everybody else. It's only been on January 7 for a few years, though. Before that, it was on January 6. *Then* they were celebrating Christmas on the same day that many other Christians were celebrating Epiphany.

The irony of this is that the holy days of Christmas and Epiphany and the dates of December 25 and January 6 have been intertwined in a complex dance for a very long time. Today, almost all Christians accept December 25 as the *date* Jesus' birth ought to be celebrated. But because of calendar differences, some Christians celebrate his birth on a different *day*. Long ago, Christians were even more divided. They celebrated Jesus' birth on different *dates* as well as different *days*.

Blame the cultural divide between East and West, the "old world" and the "new world" of the ancient world. This divide existed throughout the Roman Empire. It influenced the early Christian church and eventually led the church to the split into two major branches, one Roman Catholic, one Orthodox, in 1054. The "old world" of the East was where civilization started: in Egypt, Palestine, Syria, Asia Minor, and Greece. Greek was the common language of the East. The "new world" of the West was based in that relatively new world power, Rome. It included Italy and parts of southern Europe and north Africa. Latin was the common language of the West.

Do you think these two worlds shared the same calendar? Of course not. But the churches of East and West arrived at different dates for Jesus' birth more because of cultural differences than calendar differences. They simply approached the problem differently.

The problem is that, according to the gospel of John, Jesus died on the 14th day of the Jewish month of Nisan. The Jewish calendar is lunar; the calendars used by Eastern and Western churches were solar. So the lunar date had to be translated into a solar equivalent. Western minds approached the problem historically. They concluded that in the year Jesus died, 14 Nisan was 25 March on the Julian calendar. Easterners accepted the 14th day of their month of Artemisios as the solar equivalent of 14 Nisan. And 14 Artemisios is 6 April on the Julian calendar.[22] Add nine months to 6 April, and you get 6 January.

So, by the fourth century, December 25 was celebrated as Jesus' birthday in Western churches, and January 6 was celebrated as Jesus' birthday in Eastern churches. But, as Chryostom's pleadings show, the two sides were moving toward a sort of compromise. Basically, it was, "You accept part of *our* holy day, and we'll accept part of *yours*."

THE DAY OF HIS MANIFESTATION

Epiphany, the Feast of Manifestations, is not greatly celebrated in some churches today, especially in "non-liturgical" Protestant churches, but it is one of Christianity's earliest holy days. For many years, it trailed only Easter in importance.

From at least the time of Clement of Alexandria about 200 CE, January 6 was the day that at least some Christians commemorated the baptism of Jesus in the Jordan River. These were the followers of Basilides of Alexandria. What distinguished them from most other Christians was that they were gnostics. They claimed special "knowledge" ("gnosis" in Greek) of spiritual matters. Basilides, for instance, claimed to have learned much of what he knew from Claucias, a follower of Saint Peter. He also claimed to have gotten "secret instruction" from Jesus that was passed to him from Saint Matthew.

The basis of gnosticm is the notion that you are a spiritual being trapped in a physical body, and you will achieve freedom when you realize the truth of things. It follows that most gnostics had problems with the idea that God was physically incarnated in a fully human Jesus. God would never do such a demeaning thing, they said. We can't be sure about the full content of Basiledes's teaching because almost all reports of it come from hostile sources. But he apparently taught that Jesus attained divinity at his baptism, when the Holy Spirit descended upon him in the form of a dove and he heard the voice of God proclaiming, "You are my Son, the Beloved; with you I am well pleased" (Mark 1:11). This was the moment, Basilides said, when Jesus became Son of God.

His "adoptionist" views eventually got Basilides labeled a heretic by most other Christians, but for a time the Basilidians were simply one of the outlying branches of the growing Christian movement.

Anyway, Clement reported that the Basilidians "hold the day of his baptism as a festival, spending the night before in readings." Most accepted the date of January 6, although some observed January 10, Clement said.

We can't say *why* they thought that either date was the day of Jesus' baptism. Clement hints but never says outright that they also considered January 6 to be Jesus' birthday. Certainly Clement did. And when other Christians took up the idea, they backed it up with a familiar argument. Luke 3:23 says that Jesus was "about thirty years old" when he was baptized. True, Luke says "about" thirty, not "exactly" thirty, but the literalism of the "integral age" argument prevailed. In minds of the time, it was clear that Jesus was baptized on his birthday, January 6, nine months after April 6, the date of both his conception and his death.

The day became known as Theophany, for the Greek word meaning "manifestation of God," because it was the day the glory of Jesus was first revealed to the world. It also was known as Epiphany, for the Greek word meaning "manifestation from above." (The East/West distinction remains to this day. Orthodox churches, oriented to the East, call it Theophany. Churches from the Roman Catholic tradition of the West call it Epiphany. Epiphany is what we'll continue to call it here, too, because it's the more familiar term in the West.)

Churches throughout the East gradually made Epiphany into a unitive feast celebrating the entire story of the incarnation of God in Jesus. It particularly focused on four manifestations of Jesus: his birth, his baptism, his revelation to the Magi from the East (Matthew 2:1–18), and his display of power in the miracle of turning water into wine at the wedding at Cana (John 2:1–11). Epiphany thus became the winter counterpart to the spring festival of Easter. Since at least the second century, Easter had been a unitive feast marking several themes, including the death and Resurrection of Jesus.[23]

Ephraeum of Syria, a poet and hymnist who died in 373 CE, suggests the joy of the Epiphany festival in a liturgical reading:

"The whole creation proclaims,

The Magi proclaim,

The star proclaims,

'Behold, the king's Son is here!'

The heavens are opened,

The waters of the Jordan sparkle,

The dove appears:

'This is my beloved Son!'"[24]

Epiphany was a major event in Jerusalem and Bethlehem by 380 or so, when the Western pilgrim Egeria spent some time there. She describes a procession on the night of January 5 to the cave in Bethlehem where Jesus was said to have been born. By dawn of the 6th, they were back in Jerusalem, at the church built over Jesus' tomb, to celebrate his baptism and presentation to the world as Lord and Savior.[25]

By the time of Egeria, celebration of Epiphany was spreading West and celebration of Jesus' Nativity on December 25 was spreading East. As the Nativity moved East, it pushed the celebration of Jesus' birth out of Epiphany. As Epiphany moved West, it became more concerned with the visit of the Magi and less concerned with the baptism and the miracle at Cana.

The Nativity and the Epiphany eventually became the bookends of a twelve-day festival, made authoritative for all churches by the Council of Tours in 567. However, members of the Armenian Apostolic Church still keep the old tradition of Theophany as a unitive feast. They celebrate the Nativity and the Theophany of Jesus on January 6. (And, sticking with the old Julian calendar but following the newer tradition of two feasts, Russian and Jerusalem Orthodox celebrate the Nativity on January 7 and Theophany on January 19.)

That's the story so far: Starting from different places but using parallel logic, Christians of East and West arrived at different dates for the Nativity. The question remains whether the choice of either date had anything to do with a competing pagan holiday.

'FACTS' THAT ARE NOT SO

You will frequently read that Christians in Egypt stole January 6 from the pagans, just as Christians in Rome stole December 25 from the pagans. After all, it is said, January 6 was the winter solstice in Egypt, just as December 25 was the winter solstice in Rome.

Except that it wasn't. Eduard Norden, a "history of religions" scholar, announced in 1924 that he had found evidence of an ancient pagan winter solstice festival in Egypt on January 6. His conclusion stood as uncontroverted fact for more than 60 years and is still cited in most standard histories of Christmas and Epiphany. But another scholar, Thomas Talley, became concerned that he could find no mention of such a festival in any ancient literature. So he rechecked Norden's math—the sole basis of Norden's theory—and found several basic errors. Talley concluded: "I now understand why so many historians seem not to know that January 6 was an ancient Egyptian solstice festival. They do not know it because it was not so."[26]

Well, if there was no solstice festival on January 6, maybe there was something else even more sinister going on. The heresy hunter Epiphanius certainly thought there was. Epiphanius was a bishop of Salamis on the island of Cyprus who lived from about 315 to 403 CE. His name can be translated "clear revelation," and he tried to live up to that name by shedding light on the darkest heresies of his time. But he is not always a reliable witness. His multi-volume *Against Heresies* is a huge compendium of eyewitness reports, jumbled quotations from other works, and pure gossip.

Epiphanius was sure that some heathenish festival occurred in Alexandria on January 6, but the account he gives of it is vague and confusing.[27] To some, it suggests a goddess named Kore giving birth to the god Aeon. But the Greek word "kore" means "maiden," and "aeon" is a gnostic label for Jesus. What Epiphanius was reporting may not have been a pagan ritual at all but a Basilidian celebration of the Nativity, when the Virgin Mary gave birth to Jesus!

Epiphanius also is the chief source for the story that on January 6 the waters of the Nile River turned into wine. It's certainly a curious twist to the story from Exodus of the Nile turning into blood. Epiphanius seems to link this tale to the story of Jesus turning water into wine at the Cana wedding feast. Naturally, some commentators want to see this as the true origin of the Epiphany feast. But it's far too late. The Cana miracle was the *last* manifestation added to the Epiphany festival, not the first, so it couldn't have been the source of the feast. Anyway, a report from Chrysostom demystifies the story. He says that in Antioch, on the eve of Epiphany, river water was blessed for use in baptisms and other rituals the rest of the year—and, like good wine, the water only improved with age. It's a nice allusion to the Cana story, but it implies no miracle or parallel to a pagan ritual.

Epiphanius also is the earliest known source for the notion that Christians in Rome chose to celebrate Jesus' birth on December 25 because it was Saturnalia. Epiphanius apparently thought that in Rome the winter solstice was called Saturnalia, because he reported that the "idolaters" of Rome celebrated the birth of Jesus then. Certainly Saturnalia was a major influence on how Jesus' birth came to be celebrated (as we will see shortly). But Saturnalia ran from December 17 to 23. It was never celebrated on December 25. Epiphanius was simply confused. If Christians had set out to steal Saturnalia, they would never have chosen December 25 for the date of Jesus' birth.

Then there is the testimony of Jacob bar Salibi. Jacob (he was also known as Dionysius) was a Syrian bishop who died in 1171. He is apparently the chief source of the notion that Christians stole December 25 from the pagans. Specifically, he is quoted as saying:

> "The Lord was born in the month of January, on the day on which we celebrate the Epiphany; for the ancients observed the Nativity and the Epiphany on the same day, because he was born and baptized on the same day. . . . The reason for which the Fathers transferred the said solemnity from the sixth of January to the 25th of December is, it is said, the following: it was the custom of the pagans to celebrate on this same day of the 25th of December the feast of the birth of the sun."[28]

According to some historians who are predisposed to believe this account, that settles it. But there are at least three major problems with this text.

- One: it comes awfully late—some 845 years after the alleged theft occurred. It is, therefore, not a primary witness, but a secondary source at best.
- Two: The bishop is hardly an unbiased source. He is Orthodox, and he writes a little more than 100 years after the great schism with Rome. Note, for example, that he assumes the perspective of the East, where the Nativity and Epiphany were originally celebrated together on January 6. Like Epiphanius, he is trying to belittle Western customs by tying December 25 to pagan practice.
- Three: The quoted text is not actually from the bishop. It's not part of the original text at all. It's a marginal note added by another, anonymous, hand. We have no way of knowing who wrote it or when or why.

So the much-touted testimony of Dionysius Bar Salibi turns out to be no evidence at all.

Neither the Eastern celebration of the Epiphany on January 6 nor the Western Festival of the Nativity on December 25 has "pagan roots."

IMPERIAL CLAIMS AND COUNTERCLAIMS

Julius Caesar proposed calendar reforms in 46 BCE, and a year later Rome adopted the calendar that bears his name to this day. Eastern provinces of the growing empire didn't adopt the Julian calendar until 9 BCE, and they added a wrinkle. To curry favor with their new emperor, Augustus Caesar, they set his birthday, September 23, as the first day of their new year.

Inscriptions on marble pillars proclaimed how appropriate it was that each year begin on the date of his nativity. For Augustus, "the exalted one," was the savior of the world. He had put an end to war and brought the Pax Romana, the peace of Rome. His epiphany exceeded all previous expectations and could never be surpassed. The birthday of this god was the beginning of good news to the world that existed because of his good will.[29]

Against the imperial claims of the Caesars, Christianity made bold counterclaims. God is Lord of heaven and earth, not Caesar. Jesus is Lord, not the emperor of Rome. Jesus is exalted at the right hand of God and is Wonderful Counselor, Mighty God, Everlasting Father, Prince of Peace. He is Savior of the world, and his Nativity is the beginning of the gospel, the good news that is for all people of good will.

Constantine saw the light.

"I am the light of the world," Jesus said (John 8:12), and the Roman Emperor Constantine saw and believed. He saw that the pagan world was about to be eclipsed by Christianity. He believed that the "new world" of the Roman empire would collapse if there were not drastic change. He also may have believed, at first anyway, that the key to saving the empire was embracing a religion that merged the best of the old solar religion with the best of the new Christian way. In 321 CE, he made Sun Day the official Roman day of rest. That angered Jews and others who had been accustomed to resting on Saturn Day, but it pleased Christians, who already called Sun Day "the Lord's day." After 323, solar imagery disappeared from Constantine's coins. Had solar religion, by that time, as well?

Some poorly researched modern accounts say that Constantine "ordered" the celebration of Jesus' birth on December 25, the day of the sun's birth. But there is no record that he did anything of the kind. Events argue convincingly against the idea. It is supposed that Constantine pushed for a Nativity feast in Rome around 324, when he made Christianity a legal religion; or 325, when he assembled the great church Council of Nicaea; or 336, when the Philocalian Calendar makes its first mention of a Nativity feast in Rome. But Constantine was not in Rome any of those years.[30] He was either on the battlefield or working to establish his new far Eastern capital city of Constantinople. Funny thing about that, too. The "City of Constantine" did not embrace the new holy day until 379, more than forty years after Constantine died. You'd think an emperor would have had more clout than that, if he was really pushing something.

Obviously, when Christians started to celebrate Jesus' birth on December 25, they were aware of competition from the Birthday of the Unconquered Sun, Sol Invictus.

De solstitiis (*On Solstices*, perhaps around 380) said: "But they also call it the birthday of the unconquered. Who, surely, is so unconquered as our Lord who triumphed over death? Assuredly, what they dedicate to be the birthday of the sun is himself the sun of righteousness of whom the prophet Malachi said: 'To you who fear his name the sun of righteousness shall rise and healing is in his wings.'"[31]

Ambrose of Milan (340–397) said: "Well do Christian people call this holy day, on which our Lord was born, the day of the new sun; and they assert it so insistently that even Jews and pagans agree with them in using that name for it. We are happy to accept and maintain this view, because with the dayspring of the Savior, not only is the salvation of mankind renewed, but also the splendor of the sun." [32]

Long after pagan worship had been abolished, Pope Leo the Great (who died in 461) still had to caution that December 25 honored the birth of Jesus, not the rising of the new sun. "The festival has nothing to do with sun worship, as some maintain," he said.[33]

The festival that the Emperor Aurelian established in 274 had *everything* to do with the sun—and maybe with competing with Christians as well. Aurelian had no love for Christianity. He seems to have been preparing to move against it about this time, but then he was assassinated by some of his generals. We don't know how long celebration of Sol Invictus continued after his death. (Emperor Theodosius I abolished pagan rites in 390 CE, but that may have only forced the celebration underground.) But we also have no record of any customs associated with the festival, nothing that could have "rubbed off" on the Christian celebration. Beyond the obvious coincidences of the date and solar theme, there is no reason to suspect that Sol Invictus had any effect on the festival of Jesus' Nativity. Yet some insist on calling Aurelian the "Father of Christmas" because his festival is allegedly the origin of the date of Christmas!

Look at the chronology:

- AD 221: Julius Africanus says Jesus was born on December 25.
- AD 274: Aurelian launches the solar birthday party on December 25.
- AD 313: Constantine begins to legalize Christianity.
- AD 336: The Philocalian Calendar offers the first evidence of Christians actually *celebrating* Jesus' birthday on December 25 (as well as the first mention of Aurelian's solar birthday party).

It's a long time between 221 and 336, but the gap is easily explained. Given the potential threat of persecution, Christians didn't feel comfortable holding a public celebration of Jesus' birth. They celebrated in private and didn't go public until *after* Constantine made such celebration legal.

What we know is too sketchy to draw a firm conclusion about who stole what from whom. There is no evidence that Aurelian stole the date from Christians. *Neither is there any evidence that Christians stole it from Aurelian.*

What is much more likely is that Christians arrived at the date of December 25 independently of Aurelian. Long before Aurelian established his solar festival, Christians had what they thought were good reasons to celebrate Jesus' birth on December 25.

Whether Christians started the festival to counter Aurelian, or continued to celebrate after Aurelian moved to counter them, or started to celebrate only after Constantine made it safe, they still had the same goal. They wanted to show the empire that it was wrong. God is Lord; Caesar is not. And if saying that meant fighting over who owned the date of December 25, then so be it.

Chapter Three

Old Style/New Style

We have acquitted the Christian church of the theft of the date of Christmas. Or at least we have failed to convict it, for lack of evidence. It seems clear that the church arrived at the date of December 25 for celebrating the birth of Jesus independently of pagan tradition that set the birth of Sol Invictus on the same date.

However, once it accepted this coincidence, the church was eager to exploit it. Church leaders may not have *set out* to steal the pagan holiday, but soon they saw in it a grand strategy for evangelizing the pagan world by co-opting pagan festivals and Christianizing them.

Augustine of Hippo thought of it in terms of "plundering the Egyptians." The notion comes from the story of the Exodus of the Israelites from slavery in Egypt. After being devastated by the 10 plagues, the Egyptians were so eager to see the Hebrews leave Egypt that they freely gave away clothing and fine jewelry. "And so they [the Israelites] plundered the Egyptians," Exodus 12:36 says.

Augustine thought this was the attitude Christians should take toward any positive contributions made by pagans. "Whatever has been rightly said by the heathen, we must appropriate to our uses," he said. "Just as the Hebrews plundered the Egyptians, so should Christians plunder the heathen."[34]

Especially after 390, when Emperor Theodosius outlawed pagan worship, such "plundering" sometimes took the form of converting pagan temples to Christian worship.[35] It was only fair play. Pagan temples had stood for nearly 200 years in the places where tradition said that Jesus was born, as well as where he died and was buried. These temples had been erected not by the Emperor Aurelian but by Hadrian (who built that famous wall in Britain). In the cave where Jesus was born in Bethlehem, Hadrian built a shrine to Adonis, consort of the love goddess Aphrodite.[36] In Jerusalem, Hadrian built a temple for Aphrodite herself over the site now occupied by the Church of the Holy Sepulchre.[37] Starting in Constantine's time, places of Christian worship replaced these pagan worship sites.

This practice was encouraged in a letter that Pope Gregory the Great wrote in 601, to another Augustine, a missionary to Britain who became the first archbishop of Canterbury. Gregory said that Christians ought to turn pagan temples and customs to the glory of God by investing them with new meaning. In this way, he suggested, pagan minds could gradually be tamed and changes of attitude that could not be accomplished by leaps could be done in small steps.[38]

In this manner, the Christian church, which started with few popular customs of its own, was greatly enriched by the inheritance of a myriad of local and ethnic traditions. But the stage was set for centuries of misunderstanding and abuse.

It took generations to actually invest the pagan traditions with new meaning. Recent converts found it very easy to adopt a Christian veneer, following church precept on the surface while still revering pagan practices within. Eventually the pagan meaning of these traditions did fade from popular memory—but by then the festive customs had taken on a life of their own. As successful as the strategy proved to be, it had a visible cost. In appropriating the festivals of pagan religions, Christianity absorbed many of their trappings.

It's easy to see why the strategy would be so attractive in fourth-century Rome. Pagan Rome took a big chunk of December off each year for a huge party that started with the Saturnalia festival and concluded with a New Year's celebration. Everybody had the time off, so Christians were free to hold their own competing celebration.

Celebrating Jesus' birth at the same time had both practical and spiritual considerations. Practically, it kept Christians away from pagan celebrations. It also provided an alternative for any pagans who might be curious enough to inquire what the Christians were up to. Spiritually, it spoke to believer and unbeliever alike. To believers, it said: Never mind what pagans do on this day; we have our own reasons for celebrating. To unbelievers, it said: While you are celebrating the birth of the sun, we are celebrating the birth of the one who created the sun. A new light is dawning to illuminate a world in darkness! Come see what you're missing!

Still, the consequences of the strategy were considerable.

Some Christians got so carried away with the sun analogy that pagans mistook them for sun worshipers. Clement of Alexandria spoke of Jesus driving his chariot across the sky like the sun god, and one early painting in a tomb under the Vatican in Rome actually places Christ in the chariot of Helios. And didn't the Lord's Day (recognized as such from the time of the Apostle Paul), fall on Sun Day?[39]

To some extent the sun/Son confusion was natural, for Christians had always viewed Jesus as the true Light of the World. Moreover, it was a confusion that had been encouraged by the Emperor Constantine, who realized that the old pagan world was on the verge of falling apart and may have hoped to hold it together somehow by fusing elements of sun worship with Christianity.

The identification of Christ with the sun was typical of the problems that arose because of the absorption of pagan holidays, and it greatly distressed some church leaders. Yes, they patiently explained, the prophet Isaiah did speak of the glory of the Lord rising like the sun over Israel. Yes, the prophet Malachi did speak of the sun of righteousness rising with healing in its wings. Yes, the holy man Simeon did hail the infant Jesus as a light to the Gentiles—and, yes, we do celebrate *Sun Day* as the Lord's Day. But don't take the sun imagery so seriously that you can be confused with idolaters!

Less dire but equally serious warnings were issued about the observance of certain pagan customs. Evergreens and festive candles were common decorations during the Saturnalia and Kalends celebrations. Some church leaders were horrified when Christians, too, decorated their houses with greenery and lights. This was hardly a new concern. Tertullian of Carthage had railed against such things as early as 200 CE, long before Christians publicly celebrated the birth of Jesus in the same season. "You are a light of the world and a tree ever green," Tertullian said. "If you have renounced temples, make not your own gate a temple."[40]

When large numbers of believers started to join in the general merriment that still prevailed in late December, church leaders responded by declaring the season a period of fasting. Their protests were widely ignored. It is not so hard, the church quickly learned, to get people to adopt a new religion. It is almost impossible to make them drop customs that they had observed all their lives. If the church was going to celebrate at or near pagan holidays, it was going to have to contend with the customs associated with the holidays.

TIME IS A THORNY ISSUE

Because of their common origin, the feasts of the Nativity and the Epiphany (or Theophany, as it was better known in the East) remained confused for some time. Calendar changes contributed more confusion. The Roman world for centuries followed the Julian calendar. As we noted earlier, the calendar fostered by Julius Caesar had an unfortunate flaw that caused it to lose time. The Julian calendar's inaccuracies meant that Jesus' birthday never actually was celebrated on the winter solstice. Although the Julian calendar placed the solstice on December 25, by the fourth century the celestial event had slipped to December 21. By 1582, when Pope Gregory XIII decided to take action, the solstice actually fell on December 11.

Gregory's revised calendar solved the synchronization problem by adding a leap year with an extra day every four years. But it was a bitter pill. To adopt it, you had to make up the lost time by skipping ahead ten days. A lot of people didn't like the idea of "losing" this much time, so for centuries the world continued to be divided by differing calendars.

When Britain finally adopted the new calendar nearly two hundred years after Gregory's reform, the difference between the Julian and Gregorian calendars had grown to eleven days. By this time, the English were celebrating Christmas at about the same time other countries were celebrating Epiphany. In England and America, 1752 was a very odd year: September 2 was followed by September 14.

Many people fought the change—even after 1800, when the difference between the Julian and Gregorian calendars was a full twelve days and the day that would have been Christmas *before* the calendar change was Epiphany *after* the change. Epiphany thus acquired a new title: "Old Christmas," because January 6 "New Style" was when Christmas would have been celebrated "Old Style."

Stalwarts pointed to the Glastonbury Thorn, a tree that was said to always bloom on Christmas. In 1752, more than 2,000 people kept vigil one cold morning in a Buckinghamshire village. Sure enough, the legendary tree failed to bloom on Christmas "New Style"—but it did bloom twelve days later on Christmas "Old Style."[41]

Like the English populace, the tree had been trained one way and had to be retrained.

CUSTOMS FADE SLOWLY

The fact that such retraining was necessary gives you some idea of the great persistence of customs associated with Christmas. If the date was so ingrained that "moving" it caused such a stir, imagine how solidly entrenched were the traditions that made the date memorable.

Some of these traditions were harmless in themselves, but the sheer number of them were enough to overwhelm the celebration of Jesus' birth.

The Roman feast of Saturnalia lasted seven days, starting December 17. Only the first day of the feast had any religious meaning. After due respect was paid to Saturn, god of the harvest, the party began in earnest. Drinking, dancing and street revelry were common. If you want a modern parallel, think of Mardi Gras in New Orleans. Now let your imagination run riot. *That* was Saturnalia.

The neat and orderly world of Rome was turned inside-out and upside-down. Gambling, normally discouraged, was allowed. Class distinctions were ignored. Masters served their slaves. Debts went uncollected. Gifts were exchanged, and homes were decorated with greenery and candles. In a culture based on the reciprocity of giving, failing to join in the common jollity was a grave social error.

The birthday of Sol Invictus followed on December 25 (celebrated, after 274, if it actually *was* celebrated, in ways that are not recorded), and then people paused to catch their breath. On December 31, the revelry started up again, this time celebrating Kalends, or new year. This celebration went on for five days. Finally, exhausted and broke, Rome rested.

Of the Roman Kalends festival, the Greek commentator Libanius made these remarks, which could be applied to twenty-first century America as well: "The impulse to spend seizes everyone. He who the whole year through has taken pleasure in saving and piling up his pence becomes suddenly extravagant."[42]

If the Roman Saturnalia and Kalends festivals had been all that the Nativity celebration had to compete with, it might still have come through relatively unscathed. But everywhere Christianity went in the Roman Empire, it was the same story: Nearly every country had its own winter festival. Some countries had picked up the habit from occupying Roman troops;

others had their own ancient traditions of riotous celebration at the winter solstice.

The church's restrained Nativity celebration was easily overshadowed by the vitality of customs remembered from the old pagan winter festivals. For the masses there was never much question about which concept of the holy day would win favor. It's not that the church didn't recognize the problem and try to meet it directly. It blanketed the solstice season with saint's days and with festal tides—Advent, a period of solemnity to prepare everyone for the coming of the Christ, and the Feast of the Twelve Days to bridge the time between Nativity and Epiphany. The church also gently but firmly discouraged those pagan traditions that it considered unwholesome and consciously adopted the traditions that it found acceptable. To these traditions, it attached Christian meanings.

Evergreens, for example, figured in pagan festivals because their leaves didn't drop off in the winter. They were a natural symbol of hope for the return of spring. For Christians, they became a symbol of the everlasting love of God. But if evergreens and other wholesome customs were transformed, the essential nature of the solstice season never changed. Today, as it has been for more than two thousand years, the winter solstice is a season of frivolity.

NEW HOLIDAYS, OLD TRADITIONS

The day celebrating Jesus' birth isn't the only Christian holy day affected by association with pagan holidays and customs. Consider Halloween and Easter, both of which have come under attack, from different quarters, for their alleged pagan origins.

The "popular" history of Halloween has it originating in an ancient Celtic harvest festival called Samhain (pronounced something like "saw-wen"). Celebrated on October 31, it is said to have been a time of partying and mischief caused by evil spirits. We actually know very little about it, and that lack of information has left the door open for plenty of speculation, much of it specious. Some "conservative" Christians contend that Samhain was "an ancient pagan festival of the dead." They argue that Halloween was created to counter Samhain, and this strategy failed miserably. If that argument sounds familiar, you might suspect that it is no more true of Halloween than it is of Christmas.

The name "Halloween," of course, is a contraction of "All Hallow's Eve." That's the eve of All Saints Day, or All Hallows Day, as it was popularly known in Britain. As with Christmas Eve and the Easter Vigil, the celebration of All Saints Day began with a service the night before, on All Hallow's Eve. With All Souls Day on November 2, it formed the feast of Allhallowtide.

All Saints Day began in fourth-century Rome as a festival honoring Christian martyrs. By the eighth century, it was expanded to all those remembered as saints, and the date of its observance was moved from May 13 to November 1. That move, of course, put it smack dab on top of Samhain in Britain. But the decision to move the date was not made in Britain; it was made in Rome, where there was no Samhain or anything like it. There is no evidence that any Samhain customs rubbed off on Halloween anywhere because there is no evidence of any Samhain customs at all. What appears to have happened is that various *other* customs clustered around Halloween because it was associated with remembrance of the dead.[43]

Like Christmas (as we'll see soon), Halloween went through periods of rowdiness, suppression and reappearance in domesticated new forms. Today, despite occasional reports of poisoned candy and razor blades in apples, Halloween offers a thoroughly enjoyable prelude to the winter holiday season. Younger trick-or-treaters are commonly escorted by parents, and when you answer the door, you may see neighbors from down the street whom you haven't seen since last Halloween and marvel at how much their children have grown in a year. Costumes are often creative and fun (and, at least in my neighborhood, rarely gory). Of course, seasonal candy sales are huge ($9 billion in recent years, the National Retail Federation says).[44]

The Easter season hasn't yet been taken over by its non-religious trappings, but some people fear that it might be. It is a totally religious holiday. It celebrates an event that the modern mind finds even more boggling than the Incarnation: the Resurrection of Jesus. Yet it, too, is influenced by ancient pagan customs—or so say some atheists and other detractors.

You might think that Easter would be a clear case of a Christian holiday that borrowed nothing from pagans, especially the date. After all, we *know* when Jesus died. We may not be certain about the year, but we know that he was killed on a Friday and raised on a Sunday during the Jewish feasts of Passover and Unleavened Bread. Easter is firmly anchored to a historical date.

Despite this anchor, our celebration drifts.

Passover always starts on the evening of the 14th day of the Jewish month of Nisan. The Jewish religious calendar is lunar, but the civil calendar we inherited from the Romans is solar, and the two don't quite match up. So the date of Passover jumps around on the civil calendar. The date of Easter jumps around, too, though, and the Easter and Passover seasons don't often land near each other. Why not?

First, most Christians wanted Easter to always fall on a Sunday, the Lord's Day, the day of the week on which Jesus was resurrected. To the Christian, after all, every Sunday is a "little Easter," so there is limited appeal to the idea of Easter falling, say, on a Tuesday. Fine, so why not make Easter the first Sunday after the first day of Passover? That's precisely what some Christians did for many years. But some Eastern churches, clinging to their Jewish roots, preferred to celebrate Easter on the first day of Passover. Western churches, hoping to distance Christianity from Judaism, thought this practice was entirely too Jewish. Eventually they hit upon a way to ensure that Easter and the first day of Passover would *never* coincide. Knowing that Passover always starts on a full moon, they pushed for setting Easter as the first Sunday after the spring full moon.

The matter was settled (for the Western churches, anyway) at the first great Christian ecumenical meeting, the Council of Nicaea in 325 CE. The council set the date of Easter as the first Sunday after the first full moon of the vernal equinox.

So the solar imagery rises again. The Christian celebration of Jesus' birth occurs at the winter solstice, the shortest day of the year. The Christian remembrance of Jesus' death and resurrection occurs near another cardinal point of the solar calendar, the vernal equinox, when the length of days and nights is equal.

Pagans found cause to celebrate the spring equinox, too. It's a natural time to celebrate, for the long winter is over and it appears that the whole world is being reborn. So how big is the pagan influence on our celebration of Easter? That depends on whom you ask.

You may have seen posts on social media claiming that Easter was named after the Babylonian goddess Ishtar. Sorry, not even close. Well, then, what about *Eostre*, a pagan goddess of spring? That particular tale comes from the Venerable Bede, an eighth-century English monk who is best known for his *Ecclesiastical History of the English People*. Bede's book contains some whoppers, and Eostre probably is one of them. Still, a few scholars think she may have existed, despite the lack of evidence outside of

Bede's single reference to her. It doesn't matter. Bede clearly says that Easter is simply the English name for the festival that the rest of the world has always known as Pascha, after the Hebrew word for Passover, Pesach. So even if the English name may have come from a pagan goddess, the celebration itself certainly didn't.

What about Easter eggs? Gotta be a pagan thing, right? Not at all! In the Middle Ages, eggs were hoarded during the fast of Lent, then decorated and given as gifts for Easter, when the fast was over and eggs could be eaten again. OK, what about the Easter Bunny? Despite some fanciful stories about his connection to Eostre or some other pagan deity, nobody has ever been able to explain him (or why he isn't a her). He just sort of hops into history handing out eggs. (Don't you expect him, like Bugs Bunny, to munch on a carrot and say, "Eh, what's up, doc?")

Other customs of Easter have purely Christian origin. For example, the idea of wearing new clothes and showing them off during an Easter parade arise from the tradition of baptizing converts at Easter. They wore new white clothing to their baptism on the Easter Vigil of Holy Saturday and gaily processed throughout the next week to show that they had truly put off their old lives and put on the new life in Christ.

Some critics contend that the traditional Easter sunrise service has pagan antecedents. After all, morning vigils to greet the spring sun were part of many pagan cultures. But is there anything more natural for the Christian than gathering with other believers on this special morning and watching the day appear, imagining the light slowly revealing the empty tomb on that long-ago Sunday morning?

If only Christmas could have weathered the assimilation process so well!

REFORM AND SECULARIZATION

By the Middle Ages, the Feast of the Nativity was a scandal. In church, the masses accepted the church's restrained celebration of their Savior's birth. In the streets, they went wild. The season was a time for drunkenness, gluttony, loud and lewd public behavior, and begging that bordered on thievery. Any pagan from a previous age would have felt perfectly at home joining in the holiday revelry, once he got used to calling the old gods and old customs by new names.

The church never stopped railing against the excesses of the season, but hardly anybody listened. Whatever their origin, these were *Christian* customs now. Even if they had nothing to do with the Christian holiday, they were inextricably linked to it.

Some pious souls, such as the Franciscans in Italy and the Dominicans in Germany, tried to renew the religious spirit of the Nativity by stressing the human aspects of the story and the humble nature of Jesus' birth. Such efforts did contribute to greater public piety, but they could not change the overall nature of the celebration.

Renewal followed hard on the heels of that religious revolution known as the Protestant Reformation. Some Protestants, such as Martin Luther, embraced the holiday as it existed but tried to weed out the rowdier customs and fuse the myriad of conflicting traditions into a coherent Christian whole. The Catholic Church followed a similar strategy. And because the time was ripe for reform, the celebration was tamed considerably. However, other reformers took more drastic steps.

The Puritans of England were out to purify the church, and that meant stripping it of such "popish" elements as the Christ's Mass on December 25. They noted, correctly, that no such celebration or date was mentioned in the New Testament. They noted, correctly, that the uncontrolled revelry that had grown up around Christmas was hardly conducive to religious contemplation of the sublime event. So away with it, they said. Away with the mystery plays and the figgy pudding, away with the greenery and lights, away with the Yule log and the Christmas goose, and away with Saint Nicholas, too.

At the time of the English Civil War, when the Puritans exercised their greatest political influence, the celebration of Christmas, religious or otherwise, was harshly suppressed. At first, Christmas was declared a day of solemn fasting. When that measure failed to achieve the desired results, any sort of out-of-the-ordinary behavior on December 25 was outlawed.

Puritans campaigned against Christmas for nearly twenty years, dragging uncooperative Anglican ministers from their pulpits, jailing dissenters, busting heads when necessary. In 1647, when all celebration of Christmas was abolished and even the consumption of mince pie and plum pudding was banned, rioting broke out in several British cities, and lives were lost. The public uproar may even have contributed to the Puritans' political downfall. In the streets of Kent and Canterbury, thousands chanted that if they could not have Christmas, they wanted their king back.[45]

The return of the English monarchy in 1660 ended Puritan rule and brought a revival of the old Christmas—or at least part of it. The old revelry gradually started up again, but now it lacked even a Christian veneer. Christmas became a winter festival that happened to coincide with a religious holy day, and a discredited one at that.

The connection between holy day and holiday had been broken. By trying to suppress the popular celebration of Christmas, the English reformers succeeded chiefly in separating it from its already tenuous religious underpinnings. The popular celebration of Christmas had been secularized. By 1843, when Charles Dickens published *A Christmas Carol*, the English celebration of Christmas was essentially what it is today in so many homes: a family holiday with only superficial religious significance.

A glance at the figure of Saint Nicholas shows what happened. Nicholas had been a favorite Roman Catholic saint for more than a thousand years. He had become attached to Advent, the church's "Winter Lent," an annual period of solemn preparation for the coming of Jesus. His job was to remind children that they ought to be good during Advent. On the night before his feast day early in Advent, he rewarded good children with small gifts and left switches for naughty children to warn them that they had better straighten up.

The Protestant reformers wanted nothing to do with Roman Catholic saints, so they denounced Nicholas. But they could not do away with what he had come to represent. In England, Saint Nicholas was replaced by Father Christmas, a jolly bearded fellow who went around on Christmas Eve dispensing gifts and other tokens of joy and, yes, the occasional switch. Father Christmas did not urge children to prepare themselves for the coming of Jesus. Father Christmas did not even mention Jesus. He was a thoroughly secular figure, an image dredged up from Britain's pagan past. He eventually became known as Santa Claus.

Today we may lament the candy–and–stick approach that Saint Nicholas represented, but at least we can appreciate the intent. Nicholas tried to prepare children for the proper celebration of Christ's birth. Santa, by contrast, warns kids that they'd better be good or he won't bring them gifts on Christmas Eve. The candy and stick are still there, but the motivation has changed. The gifts Nicholas brought were intended to motivate children to celebrate Christmas properly. The gifts Santa brings are more likely to be simply rewards for proper behavior. Nicholas pointed to the gift of Jesus. Santa merely points to gifts.

So the secularization of Christmas, which we are likely to lament as a modern phenomenon, actually was accomplished in English-speaking countries more than three hundred years ago. And it was accomplished not by anti-Christian zealots but by Protestant anti-Catholic zealots.

NOSTALGIC VICTORIAN GLOSSES

When they were kicked out of power in England and then persecuted as harshly as they had persecuted others, the Puritans sought refuge in the colonies of America. They brought their hatred of Christmas with them. Christmas was not a holiday in early New England. It was an ordinary day of work, and people who took any time away from their normal tasks on December 25 were suspected of celebrating something and were subject to fine.[46]

Even the Puritans saw the need for a winter festival, however, so they invented their own. Today we celebrate Thanksgiving in late November, perhaps thinking that this was when the Pilgrims celebrated it, too. But the first Thanksgiving was on December 13—suspiciously close to Christmas, don't you think? (It later moved farther away, lest anyone be confused about what was being celebrated.)

Even the Puritan holiday could not survive homogenization and secularization. Thanksgiving began as a religious festival, a day of giving thanks to God for the bountiful harvest. Now installed on the fourth Thursday of November, it remains a day of giving thanks, although the question of to whom is left open. Nevertheless, even modern secular minds find it incongruous not to give thanks to *someone* on this day. If ever a prayer is to be said before a meal, it is likely to be said on Thanksgiving.

The Puritan ban on Christmas passed away with the Puritan governments, but the English prejudice against the holiday remained throughout much of America. During the Revolutionary War, Gen. George Washington gambled that he could slip his army across the Delaware River and attack a force of Hessian mercenaries on Christmas night. Washington was from Virginia, where Christmas had been vigorously celebrated from the start, but he was well aware of the antipathy for the holiday in the northern colonies. He figured, correctly, that the mercenaries from Lutheran Germany would be celebrating Christmas in the usual fashion and would not expect an attack, for they had no experience with Puritans and could not imagine anyone giving Christmas so little thought.

The holiday crept back into public favor as immigrants from nations that were not influenced by Puritanism brought their own ideas about Christmas to the new country. By the 1850s you could attend Christmas services in Catholic, Episcopal, Lutheran and Moravian churches, but the churches of Presbyterians, Methodists, Congregationalists, Baptists and Quakers would be closed. That didn't stop the people of these congregations from celebrating Christmas. It only stopped them from celebrating *in church*.

Thanks to Charles Dickens, whose *Christmas Carol* was immensely popular in America, there was now a word to describe those who discouraged the celebration of Christmas. And if some Scrooges still expected their employees at work and their children at school, after hours people remained free to celebrate at home, with their families, in whatever fashion they liked.

The refusal of some Protestant churches to accept Christmas as a religious holiday did not stop celebration of the day. It only encouraged *secularization* of it. Ironically, it appears that the very secularization of Christmas contributed to eventual Protestant acceptance of it. The more secular it became, the less *Catholic* it appeared!

As the holiday was revived in late Victorian England and America, Christmas lost almost all of its Catholic flavor, and much of its *Christian* character as well. Soon there was little left for anyone to argue about on religious grounds. The Victorians re-invented Christmas in their own hugely sentimental but only vaguely religious image. They made it a celebration of the family, a celebration of an idealized childhood, and a time for charity (if not precisely love) to all.

Apparently, they heard only part of the angelic message to the shepherds at Bethlehem. They glossed over the part about "unto you a child is born," and concentrated on the message of "good will to all." It was a comforting and only mildly challenging message for a materialistic age.

The Victorians also re-invented the past. The Victorian Christmas was heavily nostalgic, hearkening back to the "good old days" in "Merrie Olde England," when Christmas had been celebrated "right." But in the days when England was "merrie," the word did not mean "happy" but rather "blessed." Wishing someone a "Merry Christmas" was an expression of religious sentiment. Oblivious to (or unconcerned with) the word's original meaning, the Victorians created an intricately detailed (and largely fictional) picture of a happier past when Christmas was the most delightful time of the year—and then set out to re-create this mythical moment in the present. It is no wonder that we today find Victorian prints of holiday subjects so quaint and nostalgic. They were quaint and nostalgic even when they were new—and deliberately, if perhaps unconsciously, so.

When President Benjamin Harrison erected the first Christmas tree in the White House in 1891, he called it "an old-fashioned Christmas tree."[47] How old-fashioned was it? Though the custom went back centuries in Germany, it was only 1840 when Queen Victoria and Prince Albert started promoting the custom in England.

As the holiday grew more commercialized, ministers also discovered the value of nostalgia. A popular winter sermon subject was the turning of the Christmas celebration away from its original values and how parishioners ought to rediscover the holiday's old-fashioned spirituality. In such sermons these clergy recalled a past every bit as fantastic as the ones lay people were so feverishly trying to "re-create."

The Christmas card was invented in this era, symbol of the new extravagance in gift giving. The medieval custom of caroling was revived, and the Christmas tree was raised to pre-eminent symbol of the holiday, rivaled only by that jolly fat man in the funny red suit, Santa Claus. By the 1880s the American and English celebration of Christmas was similar to the vibrant commercial enterprise we know today. Christian and secular customs were so intermingled that their origins were irrelevant. They were simply quaint customs that made the holiday such a congenial time of the year.

INVENTED HISTORY

The "revived" Christmas of the Victorians was an "invented" Christmas.[48] So, too, was the history that caused the need for Christmas to be re-invented. The Puritans spun such a splendid web of disinformation about Christmas that most of today's secular Christmas critics are unwittingly quoting the anti-Christmas propaganda of the Puritans.

Begin with a relatively simple assertion that is hard to disagree with, even if the tone of it is aggressively negative: "It can never be proved that Christ was born on December 25." This comes from Increase Mather, a Puritan pastor who was a major figure in the Massachusetts Bay Colony.[49]

Ezra Stiles, a Congregationalist pastor who was president of Yale University when he died in 1795, said the same thing, but with a little more edge: "Had it been the will of Christ that the anniversary of his Nativity should have been celebrated, he would have at least let us have known the day."[50]

Presumably both Mather and Stiles took a lot of things on faith, but when it came to the date of Jesus' birth, they required proof. In place of such proof, Mather provided a statement that we can now declare not provable because it is simply not true. "It was in compliance with the pagan Saturnalia that the Christmas holy days were first invented."

Mather was reacting against the misbehavior that often passed for celebration in the days preceding his own. He said that in such reveling, people "dishonor Christ more in the twelve days of Christmas than in all the twelve months besides." If we didn't know the context of his complaint, it would sound remarkably modern, wouldn't it? It would sound as modern as the complaint of Libanius about the Roman Kalends celebration: "The impulse to spend seizes everyone." And what would that prove except that human nature does not change much over the centuries, and that centuries-old falsehoods still stir some people to oppose celebrating the way God intervened to redeem us?

THE MIDNIGHT OF OUR LIVES

The winter solstice is the midnight of the year, that day on which the sun shines the least and seems the most distant. It is the day the sun's fire appears to be in danger of being extinguished forever. But it is the last day of waning in the annual solar cycle. On each day thereafter, the sun shines a little longer and a little stronger, until at the summer solstice in June it shines the longest and brightest before slowly retreating again.

Pinpointing the date of the winter solstice gave ancient peoples confidence that spring would return. To them it was as if the sun were being reborn. It became a time of great celebration, and for practical reasons as well as symbolic ones. The harvest was in, and the herds were fat. There was no way to preserve much of the food over the winter; if it were not eaten soon, it would spoil. And the herds were too big; there wasn't enough fodder to keep all the animals alive over the winter, so some animals had to be butchered. Some of the meat could be preserved through the winter, but much of it had to be eaten. It was a good time for a party, for fattening up before the winds blew hard and cold. It was a last bit of cheer before grim winter locked you in its icy grip.

Centuries later, under Christian rather than pagan leadership, a similar logic spurred creation of the carnival season before Lent. The strict fast laws of the Middle Ages required that meat, eggs and milk products were not consumed during the 40 ordinary days of Lent. If they weren't to be wasted, they had to be eaten—and so they were in the week before Ash Wednesday, in a binge that concluded with Fat Tuesday, or Mardi Gras.

We misread our own inner selves, I think, if we view these times of gluttony as aberrations or moments of sin. They persist throughout the ages because they are important to us. Even today, when our warm homes and warm cars insulate us from the cold and electric lights make the night almost as bright as day, we also feel the darkness of the winter solstice. We complain about the shorter days, about how we drive to work in the dark and drive home in the dark and never see the light of day. We feel hemmed in and restless.

Even though we know that spring will come again, we fear that it might not come soon enough. How many cold days must we endure before spring returns? How many cold nights will we huddle against the wordless fear that we will never be warm again? What we need is something to take our mind off winter, something to give us hope. A party would help. We can get together with friends, eat too much and laugh away the cold. If we don't, winter can be a grim season, indeed.

Just as the winter solstice is the midnight of the year, Christians believe that God's Son entered the world at the midnight of civilization. God's Chosen People, the Jews, were being ground to dust under the heel of Roman troops. Although still invincible, Rome's empire was at its zenith and already wracked by the internal forces that eventually would cause it to crumble before barbarian onslaughts. Paganism had crested, too, for many people had discovered that it was intellectually hollow and were searching for real answers to the age-old questions. The time was right, Christians would see later, for God to make God's self known in a new way.

And so in tiny Bethlehem of Judea, a male child was born to a virgin named Mary, who was married to a carpenter named Joseph.

The child was born at midnight, so tradition says.

On the midnight of the year.

At the midnight of history.

"The hopes and fears of all the years are met in thee tonight."

Perhaps Jesus was not really born at midnight on the winter solstice. But in our minds and souls, that is precisely when he *is* born. He meets us at our lowest point, when we realize that we cannot do for ourselves what must be done. He drives away our fears and fulfills our hopes at the midnight of our lives. For us, the winter solstice is the best time, and the only time, that Jesus *can* be born.

THE PRICE OF VICTORY

It is misleading to speak, as some opponents of the Christmas celebration are wont to do, of "the pagan origins of Christmas." Christmas does not have pagan origins. It was always a Christian religious feast with the highest spiritual aspirations. Many Christmas *customs*, however, *do* have pagan influences. But this does not mean that Christmas has in any way been paganized, for the customs no longer have the meaning they had under paganism. Indeed, the origins of many customs are so obscure that no one can say for sure where they came from, let alone what they may have meant originally.

The early church assimilated these customs on the theory that they could be given new Christian meaning—or turned to the glory of God, as Pope Gregory the Great explained. To some extent, this strategy has been very successful. The original pagan meanings of the customs have been forgotten, so that if the customs have any meaning at all today, it is the meaning that Christians have assigned to them.

But there's the rub. Christmas has been so robustly celebrated for so long that its customs are now appreciated chiefly for their celebratory value. For perhaps the majority of people, even in so-called "Christian" countries, the traditions of Christmas no longer have *any* real meaning. They are simply among the things people always do at Christmas. And there are so many things to do at Christmas that the spiritual dimension of the season is often lost in the hustle and bustle.

We celebrate the winter solstice very well. But so often we cheat Christmas in the process. It is quite easy to celebrate Christmas without ever once having a religious thought. In this country and most others, Christmas without Christ is the norm.

Gregory's plan to convert pagan customs to the glory of God didn't backfire. It was simply a victim of its own success, just as Christianity has been a victim of its own success. In the Western world, Christian values are now taken for granted. By no means are all Christian values, or even the most important ones, involved. But Christian values underlie modern humanist and secular thought, as they have all Western thought since even before the Renaissance. These values are now assumed. They are so deeply a part of the Western world view that most Westerners cannot imagine life without them. They form a subtext without which the Western world view is incomprehensible.

Tragically, the subtext is now considered to be expendable. It has come to be widely believed that the religion that fostered these values is no longer of any value. We've outgrown all that, we're told. Religion was just a stage we had to go through, and now that we've learned what it has to teach us about human relationships, we can drop it.

The crisis in values that you can see every day in our society shows just how shallow this judgment is. Take away the underpinning of a value system, and the values often disappear as well.

But we don't have time to think about that now. It's getting close to Christmas and the party invitations are starting to stack up. We'd better put those decorations up in a hurry and get our gift shopping done so we'll have plenty of time to enjoy ourselves.

That's what it's all about, isn't it? Good will toward others and a happy holiday to all?

If that's *all* there is, Ebenezer Scrooge was right to say, "Bah, humbug!"

Chapter Four

Redeeming the Season

Some of the things that make the Christmas season so special to me are blends of religious traditions old and new. When our two girls were much younger, my wife and I cherished times of family worship around the Advent wreath. I remember Jennifer and Erica rearranging the figures of our Nativity scene as they told the familiar stories aloud to themselves again and again, sometimes with astonishing variations.

I enjoy singing traditional Christmas carols and listening to new Christmas music, both sacred and secular. It's a joy to soar with the delicate strains of Handel's "Messiah," swoon with the melodic outbursts of Mannheim Steamroller and rock out with Michael W. Smith's stirring anthem "Immanuel" (I like Amy Grant's version best). Christmas Eve is not complete until I have held a candle high while singing "Silent Night" during the candlelight service at church.

But many of the things that make Christmas special to me have little to do with the babe in the manger. I know that the Christmas tree has a certain religious significance, but its symbolism has only lately begun to touch me. What has moved me for many years are the memories I have of Christmas trees past. I especially remember the magically glowing trees of my childhood. (Could anything have been more wondrous?) I chuckle at the thought of the comical live tree that Linda and I chose for our first Christmas as a married couple. (Actually, it was more of a bush, and as an ecological experiment, it was a failure). Now we have an artificial tree (a concession to allergies), and each year we festoon it with mementoes of our lives together, hoping that our daughters will recall it as fondly as we recall those of our childhood.

Perhaps I would feel differently if I had been brought up to think of the Christmas tree as the Tree of Life, symbol of the sacrifice of one whose death brings life to us all. But for me it is more of a family symbol than a religious symbol. And I think most people feel the same way. To many of us, the Christmas tree is simply the most spectacular of all the season's many spectacular decorations.

For many years we have lived near Kansas City, where the Moorish contours of buildings on the Country Club Plaza are outlined each winter with thousands of colorful lights (280,000 by one recent count). Gawking at the lights while touring the Plaza by foot or car was long a winter tradition in our family. We took a horse-drawn carriage tour only once. It was expensive and required a long wait in the cold. Even more off-putting, we found ourselves less enchanted by the trip than we were worried about the safety of the horse that had to negotiate all the auto traffic. Similarly, we made only one trip to the Kansas City Repertory Theatre's annual performance of "A Christmas Carol." It was so much easier to stay at home and watch it on video (our favorite version is "The Muppet Christmas Carol" featuring Michael Caine as Scrooge and Kermit the Frog as Bob Cratchit).

I never liked company Christmas parties, but I am fond of get-togethers with friends. I love to pig out on all the goodies that people bring to even the most casual encounter. And of course the winter holidays are always times of warm remembrance of extended family, even if we usually can't manage to see everyone because of the extensive travel that would entail.

I do appreciate the spirit of giving that prevails at Christmas. I like donating to food pantries, giving away clothes that no longer seem to fit and buying gifts for families whose members I know only by size and need. As expensive and occasionally frustrating as it can be, I *like* buying presents for friends and family. I *like* preparing for the moment when we will begin sharing gifts and—I'm not ashamed to admit it—I *like* getting big gift packages with my name on them. (Small ones are dandy, too.)

So many of the things that make Christmas special to me have so little to do with Jesus. And yet I can't imagine the season without him. Obviously, millions of others can. So I have to wonder: If Jesus is essential to my celebration of Christmas, what is *not* essential? Would Christmas be Christmas without all the trappings I have come to associate with it?

The Victorians, who invented Christmas as we know it, were fond of portrayals of American and British citizens celebrating the holiday in far-off lands such as India and Africa. There is a great melancholy in these drawings and the wistful attempts of their subjects to find something in their alien surroundings that they can decorate in the familiar fashion. You can see similar scenes in photographs of soldiers on the front lines of every war in the last century, including Iraq and Afghanistan.

You can't gauge the religious feelings of the people in these pictures. You can only see their nostalgia, their longing for home. As far as you can tell, Christmas for them is all holly and tinsel, or at least the memory of it. As they gaze at some trinket that reminds them of home, who can guess whether they are seeing beyond it to an ancient sign of God's love?

Some church pastors who are fed up with the December holiday have suggested that their congregations celebrate Christ's birth in July. This way, they hope, everyone's mind will be uncluttered by thoughts of packages and decorations and everyone's spirit will be free to concentrate on the meaning of the Incarnation. I admire such attempts, but only half-heartedly, because I wonder: How will these people actually *celebrate* Christ's birth? What songs will they sing? What special things will they do? What new traditions will they create for this new holy day? Will they, in time, simply move their old traditions to the new day? Will they in the end merely be celebrating in the same way, only at a different solstice?

Can we, who have spent all our lives celebrating Christmas *one* way, celebrate it any *other* way?

MAKING THE BEST OF IT

My wife's father was born on Halloween. When Linda and her sister were young, celebration of Ed's birthday always took back seat to trick-or-treating. I'm told that he put up with it cheerfully, as he always did with the inevitable jokes spawned by a coincidence of dates over which he had no control. Thousands of others must share Ed's birth date because in recent years the greeting card companies have provided a wide selection of Halloween birthday cards. The messages range from the silly to the sick. Happy Boo-Day to you, too!

Just as celebration of Ed's birthday is colored by the association with pumpkins and goblins, so is celebration of Jesus' birthday colored by association with symbols of the winter solstice. But the birthday of Jesus has suffered even greater indignities because it is celebrated in this age-old season of merriment.

The December holiday season had existed for centuries before the Christian holy day was added to it. Only to some extent has the holy day transformed the holiday. However early and for whatever reasons Christians were led to celebrate Jesus' birth in this season, when you look back on the way it all turned out, it is easy to regret the decision. It may have been well-intentioned, and even perhaps part of a brilliant strategy for redeeming the sacred from the profane, but in some ways it still looks like an awful mistake. Couldn't Christians have found some day when the pagans weren't celebrating anything and called *that* Jesus' birthday?

On the other hand, the association with the solstice has guaranteed the Nativity celebration a lot of attention it might not otherwise get in a world that's not highly disposed to hear, let alone accept, the Christian message. Isn't it possible that the selection of the date for Christmas was not a purely human decision but one that was inspired by the Holy Spirit? (And isn't it curious that we Christians charitably attribute all decisions that we agree with to the Holy Spirit and slyly imply that decisions we don't agree with have another, more sinister, source of inspiration?)

Whatever its inspiration, I think we're stuck with the date of Christmas and, like my father-in-law, we ought to make the best of our situation.

Not every Christian would agree with this assessment. Jehovah's Witnesses, for example, do not celebrate Christmas. They spend the day as they might any other day of the year, although because it is a legal holiday they might not go to work. They cite the same grounds the Puritans did to justify their position: the date of Christmas isn't mentioned in the Bible, and most Christmas traditions don't have anything to do with the birth of Jesus. This is a reasonable position; I just don't happen to agree with it.

For one thing, I think we *ought* to celebrate the birth of our Savior. True, we have no record of Jesus telling us to mark the day of birth in any way. Neither do we have any record of him telling us to stage a celebration on the day of his Resurrection. But from all those stories he told about the bridegroom at the wedding feast, I get the impression that he would not mind us celebrating his life, for he saw everything he did as a celebration of God's love.

The question for me is *how* we should celebrate and, to a lesser extent, *when*.

It is far too late, I think, to abandon December 25. It has become the major holy day of the Christian world and one of the most important holidays on the secular calendar. As Christians, we may argue on theological grounds that Easter is just as important, even more important, than Christmas. But if we really think that we are giving too much attention to Christmas, perhaps we should try to balance the books by celebrating Easter more heartily!

Even when we celebrate it sloppily, Christmas moves us deeply. Sometimes it even moves us closer to Christ. No matter how poorly we celebrate it, Christmas still has great potential. It still can be a powerful religious experience for believers. It still can be a powerful testimony to non–believers. The opportunity Christmas gives us to open our hearts to Jesus is too valuable. We can't afford to give it up.

Remember that there are *two* Christmases, the sacred and the secular. Even if we Christians were to abandon our religious celebration of Christmas, do you think the secular world would drop *its* celebration? Do you think Santa would mothball his sleigh and put his reindeer out to pasture? Do you think the tinsel factories would close and the Christmas tree farms would grow into mighty forests? No, the season would continue to be celebrated, with us or without us. Or to put it more bluntly: *Christmas will be celebrated with Jesus or without Jesus.*

That is our choice. We can let the secular world have it, or we can find a way to use Christmas for the glory of God. We can make the worst of it, or we can make the best of it.

SANITIZING THE SEASON

The question is *how* we shall make the best of it. In what form do we want to celebrate Christmas? How should we reform it? If we don't like it the way it is, what are we going to do about it?

Some Christians are disturbed by the pagan roots of many Christmas traditions. So a logical way to reform the season might be to rid ourselves of some of the trappings of paganism that Christmas acquired long ago. Ignore for the moment *how* we might get rid of these customs. Think about which ones we might want to jettison.

Let's start with the decorations. They're pretty, sure, but what do they have to do with the birth of our Messiah? Well, not a lot—but what's wrong with decorations for a birthday party? Why shouldn't we reserve the grandest decorations of the year for the biggest birthday in history?

Evergreens are a natural decoration for a winter party. In much of the Northern Hemisphere, evergreens are about the only plant that looks alive this time of year. However, millions of people in warmer climates manage to celebrate Christmas quite well without evergreens. Perhaps those in the colder climates could get along without them, too. We can grow anything we want indoors and keep it thriving in our centrally heated homes. We go to a lot of trouble already with the fragile poinsettia, after all. We could make *any* kind of greenery a symbol of Christmas.

But why should we bother choosing another plant? What's wrong with evergreens? Oh yes, pagans used them in some of their celebrations a couple thousand years ago, and we don't want to follow pagan customs. Let's dispense with that silliness right now. Pagans also ate a lot at their celebrations. They also enjoyed themselves and laughed and hugged and kissed. Can Christians do *nothing* that pagans ever did? *Nothing* is what we would be reduced to, if we thought that we might live pure lives by doing only things that pagans did *not* do. Pagans also ate bread and drank wine. Does this mean that Christians should not celebrate Holy Communion?

If we accept the meanings that pagans assigned to things, we only honor and perpetuate their superstition. We may consider avoidance of "pagan things" a form of righteousness, but it is more likely an insidious form of Christian superstition in Puritan disguise.

God declared all of creation good. There is nothing God created that is not holy. It is only our sin that can profane what is holy. When we put something to sinful use, it is profaned. When we put something to God's use, it is holy. It is our attitude and intention that have meaning, not the thing itself. Pagans thought that evergreens were somehow magical because evergreens did not wither in winter; they considered evergreens a good-luck charm. If we don't think evergreens are magic, we don't need to worry about them. If they must symbolize something for us, they can stand for the love of God, which is everlasting and never fades.

Holly, ivy and mistletoe have more specific meaning and a checkered history as well. These evergreens were discouraged by the early church as symbols of the Saturnalia, later were merely frowned upon and finally were grudgingly accepted into church practice. Together, holly and ivy imply unity; holly is the male principle and ivy the female. As the old carol "The Holly and the Ivy" explains, the prickly holly leaves remind us of Christ's crown of thorns and the red berries represent his blood. In one verse of the carol, ivy clearly stands for the Virgin Mary. Today it is more often known as a symbol of fidelity, because it clings to things so tenaciously.

Mistletoe is now widely viewed as a generic symbol of love. The custom of kissing under a sprig of mistletoe may have come from the Saturnalia, or it may have originated with ancient Celtic religions. The Druids thought that this parasitic evergreen had healing powers and considered it sacred. Mistletoe was a common Christmas decoration in English churches in the Middle Ages but later fell from favor. In his tales of early American celebrations of Christmas, Washington Irving noted that mistletoe was considered appropriate for decorating the home but not the church. Some people still make this distinction, although it seems rather odd. Why should something be wrong for the *communal* church and yet right for the *domestic* church? How can something be wrong for one part of God's community but right for another part of it?

If mistletoe offends you, perhaps because of its association with kissing, go ahead and scrap it. But I wouldn't count this as a major victory.

Now for the biggest holiday decorations: the Christmas tree and the lights. Some pagans probably did revere the evergreen tree. They may even have set up a tree in their homes as part of a family shrine or altar; the evidence is pretty sketchy here. More thoroughly documented is the evergreen tree's link with Christmas—and that is thoroughly Christian.

In medieval Germany, most common people learned their Bible stories in the streets, in plays put on by roving bands of performers. These plays were banned about the time of the Reformation because some of them had gotten too boisterous, but the memory of them remained vivid in many people's minds. Especially memorable was the play about the Garden of Eden, performed on the feast day of Adam and Eve, December 24 on the old church calendar. A prominent feature of the play was the Paradise Tree, a fir tree hung with apples.

The tree played a dual role. First, it represented the Tree of Knowledge of Good and Evil, from which Adam and Eve ate in defiance of God's command. Second, it represented the Tree of Life, from which Adam and Eve did not eat but on which Jesus died to redeem their descendants from sin. So the play closed on a positive note: God's promise of salvation in the babe whose birth would be celebrated the next day.

Even after the play was no longer performed, people remembered the tree and its association with Christmas. They began putting small evergreens in their homes on December 24 and decorating them with apples and, later, with cookies or crackers baked in the shape of Christian symbols. Tradition says that Martin Luther came up with the idea of adding lights to the tree because they reminded him of the stars in the heavens. Luther maybe wasn't the first to light candles on his tree, but he apparently did like the idea. And from this simple notion has evolved the gaudy displays we see today in homes and businesses.

I vote for keeping the Christmas tree. Its association with Christmas is too close to sever without strong grounds, and I can't see any, other than the simple desire to be different from everyone else. What I think we need to do is educate everyone to the tree's Christian meaning. It is not simply a grand decoration. It is a grand symbol of God's plan, existing from the beginning of time and fulfilled in Jesus.

Many years ago I heard or read the story of a pastor who erected a large Christmas tree on the front lawn of his church. Christmas passed and the pastor removed the lights—but the tree stayed up. After several weeks, it was brown and shabby looking, but the pastor resisted pleas that he remove it. By spring, the tree was a real eyesore, and parishioners were wondering about their pastor's sanity. Then one day the tree disappeared. And on the Good Friday, the pastor dragged out a cross made from the tree and erected it where the tree had once stood. Now here was a man who understood the Christmas tree!

What about the lights? Their association with solstice celebrations probably predates even the Saturnalia. Pagans often lit candles or bonfires to encourage the sun's rebirth. But the association with Jesus as the Light of the World is so natural that doing without Christmas lights seems unthinkable. Jesus himself was fond of light imagery, as when he urged his followers not to hide their lights under a bushel but to let them shine for all to see (Matthew 5:15).

Well, you may say, lights are fine on Christmas trees and Advent wreaths and the like; it's the big outdoor light displays that seem so garish and inappropriate. Perhaps, but can't they, too, be a witness to the world? When others erect lighted Santas and reindeer for the delight of passersby, can't Christians set out lighted Nativity scenes? When others illuminate Frosty the Snowman and candy canes, can't Christians scatter lights in the trees to represent the way God scattered stars in the heavens or string lights in an outline of the village of Bethlehem, over which there hangs one bright star?

We needn't get carried away here. We aren't trying to compete with secular light displays, merely suggest an alternative. And if you consider lights a waste of electricity or just a tacky extravagance, you shouldn't feel pressured to put any up. But there is nothing inherently wrong with lights. They *can* be pretty, and they do add a festive air to the season. Nothing wrong with that, is there?

Enough about decorations for now. What other trappings of the season could we dispense with? What about those songs loosely labeled as "Christmas carols"? Most of them are religious; they're even in many of our hymnals. We can't dispose of these, for they may be the only Christian witness that many people are exposed to during the season. But, as we saw earlier, half the Christmas songs you are likely to hear are purely secular. "White Christmas" says nothing about the birth of Jesus. Neither does "The Twelve Days of Christmas." I'd be content never again to hear "Please, Daddy, Don't Get Drunk on Christmas." I also could live without "I Saw Mommy Kissing Santa Claus" and "Santa Claus Is Coming to Town." But I rather like "Rudolph the Red-Nosed Reindeer" (if only because I grew up listening to it, and it's one of the few holiday songs to which I know all the words).

You probably have your own list of songs you love and songs you hate. You'll have a hard time avoiding some of them on the radio and at the shopping malls. But at home, you can make your own recordings of Christmas music and edit out the songs you don't want to hear. (Good luck trying to get Alexa to do that for you.) But before you go too far with your Christmas "mix" recording, consider this mild dissent: Must every song of the season herald the birth of Jesus? Isn't there a place for a few songs such as "Jingle Bells" that merely extol the virtues of winter? Is there anything wrong with also celebrating the time of year in which we celebrate this blessed event?

LIMITS TO DEMOLITION

Parties are another way of celebrating the season. The company party, at which everyone was expected to get roaring drunk and do something they'd regret for the rest of their careers, is a dying institution. Concern about drunken driving and fear of liability suits have dampened this tradition considerably, praise God. But the holiday party is far from dead. You probably get more invitations than you can handle and wonder how you can avoid offending people by turning them down. The answer here is simple. If you don't think you'll have a good time at a party, for whatever reason, don't go. If you think you "must" go for some reason, plan to arrive late and leave early—and try to keep a smile on your face.

When you turn down an invitation or make ready to leave "before the fun starts," be diplomatic. Say that you have other commitments. (You aren't lying. You really do.) If you are pressed, explain what those commitments are, whether they are to spend more time with your family or to avoid situations you find unwholesome, such as excessive drinking. Express your position clearly but try not to make the host feel bad. Above all, don't take a "holier than thou" attitude. Make yours a loving witness.

There is nothing wrong, after all, with a good party. Getting together with friends and meeting new people is what good fellowship is all about. Christmas parties can be great fun and special times in which the bonds of friendship are forged and strengthened. But if you don't feel comfortable, it's time to go home.

That, I think, is key to our understanding and appreciation of all Christmas customs, whatever their origin. If we don't feel comfortable with them, for whatever reason, we ought to remove them from our lives. But if doing without them would cause us to feel a genuine loss, we should keep them.

If you've followed my logic so far, we've kept most of them. Not a very good job of demolition, was it? That's partly because we have yet to consider the traditions surrounding holiday gift giving, particularly that jolly elf known as Santa Claus. But there's another reason that ought to be obvious by now: There are no quick and easy solutions to the problems of Christmas. And maybe demolition is the wrong approach.

TAMPERING WITH TRADITION

Christians have been trying to "reform" Christmas one way or another for hundreds of years. Most Christmas traditions have stubbornly refused to be reformed. But great progress has been made. We are far from the riotous celebrations of the Middle Ages. In fact, we may be as far from that extreme as we are from the other extreme first advocated by the church.

The fourth-century Christians who created the Feast of the Nativity were worried that bawdy solstice customs would rub off on the feast, so they tried to make it a solemn occasion. They certainly were right to be worried about the feast being tainted by solstice customs. But considering the brouhaha in the heavens raised by the angels at Bethlehem, you have to wonder what they were thinking when they insisted that the celebration be so restrained. The birth of a baby is an occasion of joy; the birth of this baby should be an occasion of joy bursting the bounds of creation. Common folk sensed that, even when the church did not.

But the church insisted on solemnity—and that insistence pushed the celebration out into the streets, where popular custom took over. Only when it was obvious that popular custom had won did the church try to reshape the traditions in specifically Christian terms.

Protestant churches in America made a similar mistake when the celebration of Christmas was revived in the nineteenth century. Their refusal to accept Christmas kept the celebration out of the church and pushed it into the home, where popular custom took over. In both cases, popular custom clearly got out of hand, but at least Christmas remained a season of joy.

Maybe it's time to face this fact: These customs we inherited from generations unknown are a lot of what make the Christmas season so enchanting. As much as we dislike some of them and as much as we sometimes feel burdened by all of them, these traditions help make Christmas the wondrous time it is. And we keep them because they are important to us, for reasons we cannot fully fathom, in ways we cannot name.

Whenever we consider what changes we would like to make in the Christmas celebration, we ought to consider what deep emotional investment we, as well as others, have in it. As the Christian church learned when it tried to purge old pagan traditions, time-honored rituals are notoriously hard to eradicate. We tamper with popular tradition at our own peril. Individually we are under no compulsion to celebrate Christmas in any way except what we see fit. There are some holiday customs we are never going to like, and perhaps some we never *should* like. But we need to understand that these customs persist because they fill important needs in the lives of others. We must have good reason to publicly oppose customs that others find valuable, or we will look like the Grinch who stole Christmas. You may consider yourself a loving Christian, but if you fool around with Christmas, you're going to be viewed as a flint-hearted fanatic who's out to spoil someone else's fun. And you might even spoil your own fun in the process.

So are we then just like the ancient pagans who clung so tenaciously to their old customs? Perhaps we are indeed. Perhaps we are only human and looking for whatever solace we can find at the darkest and coldest time of the year. Perhaps we need these customs for the same reasons we need majestic church sanctuaries and colorful church rituals and richly evocative church music to help draw us away from ourselves and closer to God. And if these customs can help point us to Christ, where is the harm?

THE CHRISTMAS BIND

When he urged an English missionary to incorporate pagan customs in the life of the church, Pope Gregory the Great spoke of turning these customs to the glory of God. That is the real challenge of celebrating Christmas. We have to see through the holly and the tinsel to the real meaning of God's act and communicate our discovery to the rest of the world.

Most of the customs we have inherited from the pagans are mere window dressing. If we don't get carried away with them and don't allow them to distract us, they aren't a problem. The issue is not what elements of our Christmas celebration are of what origin. The issue is what we make of them.

Some sort of demolition may be necessary. Parts of the forest may have to be cleared so we can see the trees. There are so many Christmas traditions that you could not celebrate all of them in one season if you tried. You have to be selective, and of course you *want* to be. You want to celebrate only those customs that have meaning for you. This doesn't mean that your celebrations are static, unchanging year after year. You can add new traditions as you discover their value and drop old ones that don't seem to be as meaningful as they once did.

The point is that you are intentional about it. You don't celebrate in a certain way because that's the way you've always done it. You celebrate in this manner because that's the way you *want* to do it.

What you are trying to do is get to the core of Christmas, to its essence. You are trying to shape your celebration so that it doesn't drive you batty but instead moves you to a new appreciation of the meaning of Christ's birth. Sometimes, as when you shape a freshly cut pine tree, you have to lop off a few branches. But you don't want to hack off too many. The point is not to impoverish the experience but to enrich it.

Henry Thoreau, who went to the woods to live life deliberately, had this advice: "Simplify, simplify." That's where you start. In her book *Simplify Your Christmas*, Elaine St. James makes an important point. "Simplifying the holidays is not the same thing as organizing them," she says. "When you organize, you're just reshuffling the same heavy load. When you simplify, you actually eliminate a large chunk of it."[51]

Several resources can help you simplify Christmas. Besides St. James' book, I would recommend *The Christmas Survival Book*, by Alice Slaikeu Lawhead; and *Unplug the Christmas Machine* by Jo Robinson and Jean Coppock Staeheli. Also check out the free publications offered by Simple Giving

Works! That's an educational outfit that used to be known as Alternatives. (See *simpleliving.startlogic.com*.)

Even as you are simplifying, you want to amplify, to enhance what you keep. Without enhancement, simplification may be for naught.

Simplification is hard enough, but it can be done. Someone has suggested this strategy: Sometime in late summer or early fall, well before you're swept away in the Christmas rush, make some quiet time for yourself. Sit down with pencil and pad of paper and make a list of all the things you *have* to do to prepare for Christmas. You may find it exhausting just thinking about it, but that's part of the point of this exercise. Now make a second list. This time, write down only the things you *want* to do for Christmas. Now throw away the first list and follow the second one!

Or try a variation of this exercise. Make a list of things you *like* about Christmas. Make another list of things you *don't* like about Christmas. Do the one and forget most of the other.

People who make such lists often find that Christmas cards are high on the list of things they feel obligated to do and absent from the list of things they would rather do. If you feel burdened by the ritual or its cost, consider sending cards only to people you don't see very often. If you think that Christmas cards are an empty form of expression, consider sending brief personal notes instead.

Do either cards or notes have to be explicitly religious? That's up to you. You may not feel quite right sending a religious card to someone you know is not a believer. On the other hand, maybe you want to make a gentle witness to this friend, so you send a card that conveys the message more subtly. Not every card has to hammer the message with purple prose and stereotyped artwork.

The annual "Christmas letter," neatly "typed" and reproduced en masse, is a modern alternative or supplement to the card. But be warned: Some recipients consider such letters even more offensively impersonal than commercially produced cards. Others find them irritating because they often are filled with smug descriptions of the family's accomplishments in the last year.

(If you undertake such a project, remember that the object is not to impress people. You're not writing a resume but rather a letter to loved ones with whom you have lost daily intimate contact. So write it as if you were talking with a good friend. Make your letter bright and witty and chatty—and try to leave room somewhere to scribble a more personal message.

Give up the idea that you're going to save time with this option. The more personal touches you add, the more time and effort it's going to take.)

Perhaps another of your holiday traditions is baking cookies or making candy. If you continue to find joy in this, do it. But if it gets to get a burden, consider giving yourself a break. You can always buy your holiday sweets at a bakery or candy store. Perhaps you have always gotten great pleasure from elaborate home decorating and outdoor lighting. But if you don't find yourself in the mood to decorate and you just can't force yourself to climb that ladder to hang the lights, think about reducing your decorating to the essentials, just those elements that continue to add joy to your life. Next year, maybe you'll want to go back to the way you did things before, or maybe you'll find that you like the new way better.

It's *your* choice how you celebrate Christmas. You should not let the expectations of others rule which traditions you will uphold and which ones you will forgo. Remember, however, that you can't simply *ignore* the expectations of others and you can't force *your own* expectations on them. Shared traditions can be changed only by mutual consent. If helping you bake cookies has become a tradition for your children, you can't simply announce that you're tired of working in the kitchen so there'll be no home-baked cookies this year. You have to negotiate change, gently and carefully, and sometimes over a long period of time, to avoid hurt feelings.

Sometimes hurt feelings cannot be escaped. Christmas is always an emotional tug of war for some parents. They feel pressured by one or both sides of the family to spend Christmas Eve or Christmas Day at Grandma's house. On the one hand, these parents want to feel the warmth of another Christmas in their own parent's home, perhaps the very house in which they grew up. They also want their children to experience the joy of the holidays in the company of loving grandparents. On the other hand, they want to establish an independent tradition of Christmas in their own home, just Mom and Dad and the kids. They are emotionally torn because they know that no matter what they do, someone is likely to feel slighted. They are especially torn because they know that when *they* are grandparents, they will be making the same emotional demands on *their* children.

It's even harder when the family is split by divorce or separation. Will Mom or Dad have custody of the kids for Christmas?

Such questions are never easy to resolve. Traditional answers may not be the right ones. Be as loving and flexible as you can and pray for patience, strength, and guidance.

Some of the hardest expectations to fulfill, and the hardest to resist, are not those of your family but those of your community. So much of the pressure at Christmas comes from your friends, from your children's school and, all too often, even from your church. How easy it might be to celebrate Christmas properly, you think, if only there weren't so many demands from so many others. Christmas is such a happy time of year that everyone wants to get in on the act. Everyone wants to have a party or a program, and everyone wants *you* to contribute something to it. "I'm only asking for a dozen cookies," says the leader of the school social committee. "Yes," you reply with a sigh, "but you're the *fourth* person who asked this week!"

Schools and churches say they want to encourage family values, so they plaster the Christmas season with programs and performances. Before you know it, you're attending so many manufactured family activities that you don't have time for the natural family activities you might enjoy at home, if you were ever there, which you're not. (The intent is generally good. These programs try to supply what so many children never get at home. But they make it all the harder for parents who already make time for their children and try to make Christmas a spiritual experience for the whole family.)

At some point, you have to start saying "No!" It is never easy. And sometimes you wind up saying no to things you would *like* to do because you can't find a way to say no to things you *don't want* to do. Yes, you find yourself saying, we'd love to go caroling on Wednesday night, but we have school and club programs every other night this week and we've just got to have some time to ourselves at home.

This is the Christmas bind, and it is a terrible thing. For the one thing you need before Christmas is time: time to relax, time to reflect and time to pray. You need this time for you and your spouse, for you and your children, and just for you. You need moments of solitude as well as family time. And the whole world, it seems, is conspiring to see that you don't have it.

If you want this time, you have to build it into your schedule from the start, and you have to guard it jealously. You might, for example, reserve Sunday evenings during Advent as family time. Or you might declare the week before Christmas off-limits to all outside activities. But it is not enough to simply declare your independence from the Christmas rush. Once you have staked out this new turf, you have to defend it. Only persistence can save you from the Christmas bind. You have to be determined.

You have to be firm. You don't want others to take Christmas away from you. It's too important.

All too often, we give up too easily. It is easy to be distracted at Christmas. It is easy to get so wound up in the externals that we miss the internal celebration the externals are supposed to point us toward. But it is also easy to blame those externals for our failure to be renewed by Christ. Yes, Christmas is a busy time of year. Yes, it is hard to make room for Jesus. But can you name any time of year when it is *easy* to make room in your heart for Christ? When are you *ever* ready to do that?

Isn't complaining about the busyness of the season just an attempt to shift the blame away from our own spiritual poverty?

THE REAL CHALLENGE OF CHRISTMAS

Sometimes we feel so bombarded by Christmas that we complain that the season is too long. Perhaps the real problem for many of us is that the season is too short. How often we say, "Christmas is coming so fast!"

To think of the modern Christmas, think of a powerful magnet drawing all things to itself. Or think of a giant black hole in space sucking everything into it and squeezing it into oblivion.

The secular "holiday" season extends from Halloween to the last play of the last football game on January 1. The sacred Christmas season starts with Advent on the Sunday nearest November 30 and ends with Epiphany on January 6. Both secular and sacred seasons focus on a single day, December 25. It's no wonder so many people feel let down on December 26. No single day can live up to the expectations we heap upon Christmas. No single day can fulfill all our hopes and dreams. Disappointment is almost inevitable.

We are right to focus on that one day but wrong to focus so narrowly on it. Christmas is not one day. It is an entire season. If we celebrate Christmas as a season, we can find it less stressful, more enjoyable and more meaningful.

Christmas doesn't just happen. Even the secular Christmas has to be prepared for. The sacred Christmas also demands preparation.

Advent is our time of spiritual preparation, the time we use to make our hearts ready. The ancient church considered Advent a time of fasting, and in some of the more liturgical churches Advent still can be a rather dreary period. Don't you wish you could skip those heavy Advent hymns such as "O Come, O Come, Emmanuel" and "Come, Thou Long-Expected Jesus"? Aren't you ready from the start to sing "Joy to the World"?

Yet waiting is an important part of it. Advent is a time of hopeful waiting for the coming (the Advent) of Jesus. It is a time in which we try, with the help of spiritual exercises such as daily Bible reading and reflection, to confront the hopes and fears of all our years. But we know how this story ends! We know that our best hopes can be fulfilled in Jesus, and that God's amazing grace can help us overcome our fears. We wait, yes, and we hope—but we build joy in our hearts in anticipation of the event we celebrate at Christmas.

The last day of Advent is the season's most exciting day. Christmas Eve has become for many Christians more of a religious holy day than Christmas itself. This is a curious and wonderful reversal of the common trend in the history of holy days and holidays. In anticipation of the holy day, celebration starts on the eve. All too often, the eve becomes a riotous holiday, as is the case with All Saints' Day and Halloween. But because Christmas has so long been a secular holiday, the primary religious observance of Christmas has moved to the evening before.

Christmas Eve services are among the best-attended and most memorable events of the church year. Who is not moved when the electric lights are put out, the Christ candle is kindled and the flame from that single source is passed from person to person throughout the church until all are holding their candles aloft as they softly sing "Silent Night"?

This single moment can tell more of what Christmas is about than a hundred sermons from the pulpit and a hundred books about the meaning of Christmas. One of my most powerful memories of Christmas is from 1979, when my wife and I experienced this blessed moment while holding our first child, Jennifer, who was then barely a month old. Many of our hopes and dreams were fulfilled with her birth, and in that moment we were stirred by the possibility of even greater hopes and dreams being fulfilled with the birth of the infant of Bethlehem.

This is the moment we have been preparing for throughout the four weeks of Advent. This is the moment of Christ's birth. If we are prepared for it—and sometimes even if we are *not* prepared for it—this is the moment of Christ's rebirth within us. This moment is pure Christmas.

After this, the events of Christmas Day are almost anticlimax. Christmas is a family occasion these days. If there are children in the house, it usually means rising early for the frantic unwrapping of gifts. Afterward, perhaps a leisurely breakfast, then back to the tree to enjoy the new things we have acquired as tokens of love we find hard to express in any other way. There may be visiting of others later in the day, and caroling in some families, sledding if there is enough snow and a good hill nearby—good wintertime fun. The day passes so quickly.

When it's over, we may feel let down. We have invested so much of ourselves in this time together, perhaps too much of ourselves, and now it's over. The Day After Christmas can be the saddest day of the year. Our hopes fade, our fears return.

It doesn't have to be this way. Long ago the church declared that there were twelve days in Christmas—and if we don't celebrate every one of them, I think we're cheating ourselves.

We can't celebrate the other eleven days of Christmas as we celebrated the first one, but we can make each day special in its own right. Who says you have to do all your Christmas baking before Christmas? Do some of it now! Who says you have to give all of your gifts on December 25? Save some important ones for later! Not necessarily gifts of material things, but gifts of yourself—IOUs for hugs and special favors, and most of all the gift of time.

Find a way to spend extra time with your loved ones in these days. Shower them with the gift of your loving presence. It's hard when you have a job and sometimes you have to work extra hours because so many others have the time off. But try to save the best of yourself for those who need you the most. And take the time off yourself, if you can. This is what vacations are all about.

Give spiritual gifts, too. Make this a time of family sharing. Share your vision of what Christ's presence means in your life. Share your joy at being loved by your Creator.

Finally, on January 6, the day of Epiphany, celebrate Christ's "coming out" party. Celebrate his manifestations to the world—his showing to the Magi at Bethlehem; the inauguration of his mission at his baptism in the River Jordan; and his first miracle, the seemingly innocuous changing of water into wine at the wedding at Cana. In a few months you'll be celebrating another miracle. What you're doing now is setting the stage, marking the transition from helpless infant to empowered savior. You're closing the Christmas season. Christ is born. He is living in you now. It's up to you to live for him.

This is the real challenge of Christmas: to celebrate it in a way that renews our commitment to Christ. This is the real challenge of Christmas: to live it day by day, in all seasons throughout the year. This is the real challenge of Christmas: to make our celebration of it so vital and so meaningful and so exciting that others will want to make it theirs also.

Chapter Five

Christmas Wishes

My childhood memories of Christmas are at once comfortingly vivid and frustratingly vague. I remember waking one Christmas morning shaking with excitement. I quickly rousted my brother, and we tiptoed down the hall to the living room. It was still early, and the room was in shadows. We could make out little in the darkness except the towering mass of the Christmas tree and shapeless forms on the floor around it. We switched on a light and ventured closer.

I don't have any idea what we found under the tree. My memory stops cold at this point. Whatever we found, I am sure that we were delighted with it. We were rarely disappointed by Santa's deliveries—and not because we always got exactly what we wanted. Sometimes we did, but even when we didn't, we were happy.

Maybe our parents simply prepared us well for disappointment. I do recall being told that Santa couldn't fulfill all Christmas wishes, only some of them. I must have taken the lesson to heart. I remember one Christmas afternoon when we were visited by some friends and one of the girls in this family was still pouting because the doll she'd received wasn't the one she had set her hopes on. I was amazed. I thought: "What's wrong with her? She got a doll, didn't she?"

I know my parents tried hard to give my brother and me what we wanted, even if they also tried to shape our expectations to fit reality. One of the most cherished Christmas gifts of my childhood was an American Flyer train set. (I still have it in a box in the basement.) You have to understand that American Flyer was not my first choice in electric trains. Like every boy I knew, I wanted a Lionel train set. Still, I wasn't disappointed when I got an American Flyer. Because it was *mine*, I considered it first rate.

My parents were financially strapped in those years. They must have struggled to afford the gifts they lavished on their two boys. I thought old Santa was pretty extravagant when he visited our house, even if some kids at school could brag about getting bigger presents or more of them.

I still wonder about that one Christmas morning. I wonder why I can remember the anticipation so well but can't remember what I found waiting for me under the tree. I have so many complete memories of childhood Christmases. Why is this memory so fragmentary? Is it because the moment of discovery was more important than the discovery itself? Is it because the feeling was more important than the gift?

GREAT EXPECTATIONS

What do you want for Christmas?

What do you *expect* from Christmas?

Your wants and expectations may be worlds apart—and yet they are intimately related, for Christmas is above all a season of hope. At this time of year it is especially easy to *expect* what we want and to be bitterly disappointed when we don't get it.

Many people dread the coming of the season, and not simply because they are weary of the annual obligations of decorating, gift giving, and putting on a cheery face. They dread the season because they know it cannot fulfill their hopes. They know that certain loved ones will not be home for Christmas because of death, broken relationships, or simple geographic scattering. They know that certain cherished memories can never be relived, or even renewed. They know that lack of money will mean fewer presents under the tree, and they feel helpless in their failure to provide the happiness they seek for their families.

People are supposed to be happy at Christmas. Everyone knows that. So feelings of unhappiness are greatly intensified as Christmas draws near. The season of joy can become a symbol for all that has gone wrong in our lives.

Christmas also can be depressing when our expectations are unrealistic, when we hope for too much.

When we are very young, we can be totally delighted by a Christmas gift. A new toy can make us indescribably happy, at least for a while. When we're older, sometimes even while we're still children, life gets more complicated. No wrapped package can spark in us the childish glee that we remember so well from Christmases long past. But sometimes we *think* it can—and then, even if we get what we want, we may be dismayed to discover that it's not enough. And we wonder why we feel so empty, so unfulfilled.

We want each Christmas to be perfect. Our image of the perfect Christmas is part memory and part fantasy. Christmas memories are powerful. They also can be distorted. So often we remember the way we always *wanted* Christmas to be, the way it *should* have been, even if it never was, and then we try to "re-create" this ideal. We struggle desperately to make it happen and we blame ourselves when it doesn't.

We so love Christmas that sometimes we make too much of it. Our hopes swell to impossible dimensions. We expect wondrous things to happen. Greedy children will discover the joys of sharing. Relatives who have never gotten along will stop bickering. Barriers between loved ones will fall. Only on the Night of Miracles could we expect such things. Only at Christmas could we expect God to personally step into our lives the way God once stepped into the world at Bethlehem. Only we want *more* this time. We want a miracle that is perhaps even bigger than the Incarnation. We want God to set everything in our lives right and deliver it to us in a neat package under our Christmas tree on the morning of December 25. Sometimes we expect too much, even from God. And it hurts terribly when we don't get it.

WHAT DO YOU WANT?

What do you want for Christmas?

Think about it. What do you *really* want? A new coat? An expensive ring or other bit of jewelry? A fancy new car? Those things might be nice, but would your Christmas be ruined if you did not get them? Have you so set your heart on some *thing* that Christmas would be tragically marred if you did not get it?

Even if you are destitute and the smallest gifts might ease some of the burdens of your life, you probably realize that there is more to Christmas than material things. Indeed, if you are poor, you may understand, as a wealthier person might not, just how fleeting are material things. Here today, gone tomorrow, they are wonderful for a time, but they don't last. What you really want for Christmas is something that lasts.

Peace on earth and good will to all—that's what many people say they want for Christmas. It's entirely too glib an answer. Who doesn't want peace? Who doesn't want to bask in the glow of good will for all? But who really expects it as a Christmas gift? Long ago, God made an announcement of peace and good will—and gave us a baby. Apparently God thought the baby was enough for us.

When the baby grew up, he brought us a message of God's love, and then he died to prove that it was real. Isn't that what you really want for Christmas? Isn't that all you have always wanted? Don't you simply want the security of knowing that you are loved?

Isn't *that* what Christmas is all about?

GIFTS OF CHARITY

When we are apart from loved ones, Christmas can hurt because love seems impossible. The Christmas gift is a sign that love *is* possible. It is only a token, a small manifestation of our much larger love. But it is important because it shows that we care.

The custom of Christmas giving has gotten so commercialized that we often forget its deeper significance. The gift, the showing of love, is the essence of Christianity. It is love in action.

James, the brother of Jesus, said that faith without works is dead (James 2:17). So it is with love as well. Love is not a feeling but an action. Love that is not expressed in action is not love at all, but indifference hiding behind sentimentality.

The expression of love is the core of our faith. God showed love for us by coming into the world in the form of Jesus. Jesus, God's Son, told us that we could show our love for him by loving one another. We can love others without loving God but we cannot love God without loving others.

Jesus was the first Christmas present. Jesus was God's gift to us all, an embodiment of God's love for us. Jesus said that if we love God, we will embody that love in our actions toward others.

Christmas gifts are only a small part of it. Yet our attitude toward Christmas giving may mirror the depth of our love for others. If we are stingy at Christmas, when gift giving is socially acceptable, how generous are we likely to be throughout the rest of the year, when there are fewer social pressures to show our love for others?

It is easy to misunderstand the linkage between love and gift giving and assign it too much weight. For example, it's natural to assume that the more we love someone, the more we will want to give them. If we love someone a lot, we will want to give that person a lot. But there must be a limit to how much we give. The gift is not the full expression of our love, only one sign of it.

We can, however, come to view the size of a gift as a gauge of how much we love someone and thus totally miss the mark. For then we tend to judge the depth of that person's love for us by the size of the gift that person gives us in return. "She must not love me as much as I love her, because I gave her a much bigger gift than she gave me." Or: "He must really love me because what he gave me was so extravagant."

We want so much to be loved that sometimes we try to buy it. We think we can earn love by giving others things that will please them. But it's not the gift that shows our love. It's the giving.

What do you often say when you are given something that you think is a little odd? With an indulgent little smile, you say, "It's not the gift but the thought that counts." It's not the gift we measure but the attention the giver pays to us. Even if the giver misjudges our likes and dislikes, he has at least tried to bring us joy. The thoughtful gift will always be appreciated by the recipient, even if she already has three of them (and especially if she has never told anyone that she likes the thing, let alone likes it so much that she has three of them).

When we give a person something, we would be gratified to receive a statement or sign of appreciation from that person, some form of "Thank you"—and yet we really should not expect one. Although universally considered a sign of good manners, such a response is a gift itself. And we do not (or at least *should* not) give gifts in expectation of getting anything in return, even a sign of gratitude. A true gift has no strings attached, especially emotional ones.

Jesus said that the highest form of giving was when we had no expectation of any return from it. And Jesus said that we have to learn to give this way. Even pagans give presents to family and friends, he said. The inhabitant of God's kingdom gives to others as well. The followers of Jesus love not only those who return their love but even those who are their enemies.

In short, Christian love and Christian giving are not conditional. They are universal. Christians give not only to family and friends but to people they don't even know (and might not like if they did).

Sometimes we call this "charity," possibly because the old King James translation of the Bible uses the word "charity" where modern translations find the word "love" more appropriate. Nevertheless, charity, as we understand it today, is a part of love. Charity is giving without expectation of return, usually to people we do not know, for the simple reason that we care about their welfare.

The Christmas season has become the season of charity, the time in which we are asked to remember those who are poor and to do something to make their holiday a little brighter. In the season of good will to all, we respond with uncommon generosity to the tinkling of bells on street corners and other solicitations for aid. Some of us may do it out of guilt, or from a sense of humanitarian obligation. But at Christmas even the hardest heart may find a way to love strangers and ache to express that love with a gift. This is often known as "the spirit of Christmas." It is really the spirit of Christian love. And it was never meant to be shown only at Christmas.

FLAMING DESIRE

The custom of winter gift giving comes to us from the Roman holiday season encompassing the Saturnalia and Kalends festivals. During this season, the Greek observer Libanius reported, "People who spent the entire year hoarding their money suddenly feel the urge to part with it." Obviously some things have changed little in two thousand years!

Some fourth-century Christians may have fought it for a time, but gift-giving soon became part of the Christmas celebration. It's a natural fit. Jesus was God's gift to humanity. The Wise Men gave presents to the infant Jesus. Why shouldn't Christians give presents during this holiest of seasons as a token of their love? How quickly it gets out of hand.

If Christmas was to some extent commercial from the beginning, the heavily commercialized Christmas that we know today is barely 150 years old. It is the product of the Victorian era's revival of Christmas as a thoroughly secular holiday. The English and American Christmas of the 1880s probably seemed just as commercial as ours feels today. The major differences are that the selling season then was shorter and focused more on children, and the sales techniques of that time were primitive by our standards. The season, the audience and the sales pressure expanded greatly with the growth of mass merchandising and mass media in the first half of this century. You can chart the most recent phase of this process from the late 1930s, when the department store Santa Claus was in his heyday and such films as "Miracle on 34th Street" were released.

As distressing as this trend is, faint hope exists that it can be reversed. It is commonly believed that Christmas is getting more commercial each year—and this may be so. But what also may be changing is our attitude. Christmas may appear to be growing more commercial because our tolerance for Christmas commercialism finally is wearing thin.

If this is true, we still have a long way to go. Everyone agrees that Christmas is too commercial—even those who help make it more commercial. And who does not contribute in some way? Who among us can claim innocence?

Some of us would like to put all the blame on greedy merchants. True, retailers often promote excess consumption. They also serve our needs and feed our wants. If they didn't, they would go out of business. Why do stores start displaying gift items so early in the season? Because their customers want to get an early start on shopping. Why do stores offer the newest and the best in the month before Christmas? Because that is when shoppers want the goods. Businesses may fan the flames of consumption, but the fire is already burning brightly in our hearts and minds.

The conflagration threatens to burn out of control. Christmas accounts for one-fourth of the annual sales of many retailers in the United States. More than half the toys sold each year are sold in the weeks before Christmas. More than half of such luxury goods as furs and diamonds are sold in the last quarter of the year. Economically speaking, Christmas creates an unwieldy bulge of spending and a potentially dangerous spike of debt.

Is this, we ask ourselves each year, what Jesus would have wanted? Obviously not. Most of our Christmas spending does not go to help the poor. Most of it goes to help ourselves. Most of our giving is to family and friends. We give most not to those who need it most but to those we love most. Of all the things wrong with Christmas, this may be the most serious. It shows that we have missed the point entirely.

In the Middle Ages, it was believed that Christ returned to Earth every Christmas Eve as a beggar, and that if you refused to help a needy person you might be spurning Christ himself. As fanciful as this belief is, it rests on some solid theological ground.

Jesus said that when the time for judgment comes, the King will say to the righteous: "Come, you that are blessed by my Father, inherit the kingdom prepared for you from the foundation of the world; for I was hungry and you gave me food, I was thirsty and you gave me something to drink, I was a stranger and you welcomed me, I was naked and you gave me clothing, I was sick and you took care of me, I was in prison and you visited me."

And the righteous will ask: "Lord, when did we do these things for you?"

And the King will answer: "Truly I tell you, just as you did it to one of the least of these who are members of my family, you did it to me" (Matthew 25:31–40).

The challenge of seeing Christ in the faces of our brothers and sisters is hard enough any time of year, let alone at Christmas.

GIFT STRATEGIES

It has been described as the "Christmas Merry-Go-Round" or the "Christmas Machine." You know what it is because you've gone around and around on it and occasionally been mauled by it. You have to buy gifts for every member of your immediate family, several members of your extended family, certain close friends and a host of others, from the person who cuts your hair to your boss (or, if you're the boss, to your employees). The demand for gifts never shrinks; instead it expands each year. Your gift list is fat, your purse is thin, and you cringe each winter the first time you hear someone singing, "It's beginning to look a lot like Christmas!"

Is there any way off this runaway train, or all we all doomed to crash at the end of the line? Can't we bring some blessed sanity to the custom of Christmas gift giving? Sure we can. But don't expect it to be any easier to tame this monster than it is to get control of any other Christmas tradition. In fact, expect it to be *harder*.

If you really want to be "scared straight" on this issue, you can do one of two things. You can start at the beginning of the Christmas season and record every expenditure you make for every part of your holiday celebration, or you can sit down afterward and try to estimate how much it has cost you. Either way, you will be amazed. You will be shocked. You will be appalled. And, if you're like most people, you will immediately shove the awful thought out of your mind and make some vague promise to try to do better next year.

You won't do better, of course, unless you have a firm plan and the resolve to see it through. You need a detailed budget and a lot of will power.

A modest Christmas for a small family will cost more than $600 *for gifts alone*. A more extravagant Christmas for the same family or a modest Christmas for a larger family, could easily top $1,200, just for gifts. These are conservative estimates. Some people might consider them ridiculously low (while others can only yearn to be able to spend so much).[52]

Can your budget take a $1,200 hit without flinching? Mine can't. (And if yours can, you probably spend more than that on Christmas gifts anyway.)

Some people try to take the sting out of Christmas giving by spreading the cost out over the year, either by financing it on credit cards (bad idea) or by saving in advance through a Christmas Club account at a bank or credit union. These people know how much Christmas costs. They pay for it every month.

That modest $600 Christmas will cost you $50 a month for one year. The less modest $1,200 Christmas will cost you twice as much. If you really want to "take the cure," try keeping the record in cash. If you're saving for a modest Christmas, every morning right after you brush your teeth take $2 from your wallet and put it in a safe place. At the end of every month, deposit your $60 or so in a savings account. After a year you will have saved more than $700—and probably made yourself sick of Christmas.

Another way of spreading out the cost is to purchase gifts the year-round. This is one way we try to shop in my family, and I can testify that although this doesn't necessarily lower the cost, it can make the final weeks before Christmas less hectic and the results more satisfying. What Linda and I do is shop for gifts wherever we go, especially when we're on vacation or browsing through shops in another town. If we encounter something that we think is just perfect for someone on our Christmas list, we buy it—even if it is the middle of July.

You can't buy all your gifts this way, of course. Children never grow at even rates, so it's not safe to buy them clothes much before they need them (even if you could, given the seasonal nature of clothing sales). Toys also are hard to purchase in advance. That special toy you buy in April may be given to your daughter by someone else on her birthday in August.

The limitations of this strategy are obvious, but we have found that some of the gifts people most appreciate receiving are those special items that we discovered months before in out-of-the-way places such as craft boutiques, county fairs and museum gift shops.

Linda's parents commonly had almost all their Christmas shopping done before the end of November. Maybe this gave them something extra to be thankful for on Thanksgiving. It definitely moved the budget bulge out of December and gave them a whole month to relax before Christmas. Linda and I are trying this approach, too, and we're getting better at it.

We're still spending too much, though. It happens every year, no matter how early we wrap up our shopping. We've gotten that "perfect" gift for each person on our list, and then one of us (sometimes her, but, I confess, usually me) decides that it's not enough. We've got to get one more thing for this person and then one more thing for his wife so that their gifts "balance." And as long as we're at it, there are a couple of other things we could throw in . . . A few dollars here, a few there. Pretty soon you're talking real money!

And all we're doing is *exchanging* gifts. We're giving presents to people who will be giving presents to us. Some cynics suggest that we might as well just exchange cash and then buy ourselves what we want. Isn't that what gift cards are for? At its most mechanical, Christmas giving is hardly better than this. But it's still the thought behind the gift that counts most, and an exchange of thoughtful gifts is worlds away from an exchange of cash. (And sometimes gift cards really are the best choice.)

An exchange it remains, however. It's the affluent helping the affluent. We all know that the hardest people to buy for are those who already "have everything." So why are we buying them *anything*? Shouldn't we be giving to those who have nothing or next to nothing?

I have heard this suggestion: Resolve to spend half as much or more on charity as you do on gifts to family and friends. I think this idea has merit, but it raises some questions. If you spent $600 on Christmas gifts last year, what will you do this year? Will you keep your overall spending the same and spend $300 on gifts and give $300 to charity? Or will you spend $600 for family and friends and give $300 to charity?

Either way, you probably would be giving more to charity than you do now. And either way, you ought to ease into it. Don't try to change everything in one year but make it a goal to reach the new level within two or three years. If you spend half as much next year on presents, there may be some hurt feelings, however hard you have tried to prepare everyone for the change. And if you try to keep gift spending level but give more to charity, you may push yourself near bankruptcy.

Here, as with so many other aspects of Christmas, a delicate balance is what you are trying to achieve. You can't achieve that balance without the cooperation of friends and family members with whom you exchange presents. It may be difficult to sell some of them on the idea of simplifying their Christmas giving. However, most people feel financially pinched at Christmas and would welcome ideas for change. Here are three approaches to consider:

- Set a dollar limit on what should be spent on each gift.
- Draw names, so that you don't feel compelled to buy for everyone.
- Give presents only to the children.

Present these ideas or others of your own and talk them out with the people involved well before the holiday season approaches. You may meet some initial resistance. On the other hand, you may be surprised at how eagerly some people respond to your overtures.

Some parents have adopted a simple but strict policy of family gift giving. Children get four gifts: something they want, something they need, something to wear, something to read. It has a catchy sound, and it might provide a helpful restriction, but before implementing it, I think I'd check with other parents about how it worked for them.

If you accomplish no more than simplification, you will have worked wonders. And what about amplification? What about giving to the poor? Calculate how much you have saved and give it away. Just do it quietly. If you tell them what you're doing with the money, your loved ones may understand your motivation and applaud your generosity and even feel moved to follow your example. Or they may hate you for it. You won't know unless you tell them, and it's not worth the risk. You shouldn't trumpet your virtue anyway. As Jesus said, when you give such gifts, your left hand should not know what your right hand is doing (Matthew 6.3).

Some people will never understand charitable giving. They have heard the stories of welfare cheats and street hucksters and concluded that all needy people are frauds. Yes, some poor people do cheat, but some rich people cheat, too, and poverty is no more a sign of dishonesty than wealth is. It is no sign of virtue, either. It is merely a fact of life. Very few people are poor voluntarily. Whether we see the poor as victims of an unfair social system or victims of personal failure or bad breaks, we should not fail to love them and to help them. There will always be a few cheats. But more importantly, as Jesus said, there will always be people in need (Matthew 26:11).

If you're new at giving to charitable organizations, you may be bewildered by the number of agencies competing for your donations. There are many worthy causes—too many for your limited resources. You may wish to make a small contribution to many groups or larger contributions to fewer groups. Seek counsel from your pastor and friends. They can tell you which agencies do what kind of work and which ones have special needs you may be able to help fill.

Don't limit your contributions to cash. Many agencies need volunteers, and the gift of your time and talents may be more precious than your money—and even more of a sacrifice for you.

It is possible to "adopt" a family through some agencies. You receive a list of first names, ages, needs, and sizes. You buy gifts for this family, just as you would buy gifts for your own family. Sometimes you deliver the gifts, too. This can add a personal touch to your giving, but it is not always the best approach. Most people are acutely embarrassed to receive such generosity from strangers. You may feel good about giving the presents, but they may not feel so good about receiving them from you. Personal deliveries can be awkward for everyone involved and harmful to the receiving family's self-esteem. Ask the sponsoring agency for advice, and if you're uncertain how you will react in the situation, avoid it.

You probably recognize the boor who drags his children with him every year when he crosses the tracks to the "wrong side of town" to make his Christmas deliveries. He makes a big show of his largess to "the needy and unfortunate" and then he goes back home, where he'll stay for another year, until it's again time to take the kids in tow and show them how lucky they are to have him for a parent. He gives *something*, which is more than some people do, but his is not the kind of witness you want to emulate.

Sometimes it's best to remain anonymous. This is the example embodied in the legend of that towering figure from the fourth century, Saint Nicholas. As a priest and bishop in what is now Turkey, he encouraged the members of his flock to be faithful to God. And sometimes he bolstered their faith by leaving them anonymous gifts. When he was once discovered in the act of delivering a gift, he begged the person not to reveal his identity to others. He gave in secret so that no one would feel indebted to him.

A hint of this tradition is preserved in the German custom of Christkindl. (You may be more familiar with the tradition in its secular form, called "secret Santa" or "secret friends.") As it's commonly done, members of a family or other group draw names at the beginning of Advent. The person whose name you draw is your Christkindl, the one who represents the Christ Child to you. Throughout the weeks of Advent, you give the Christ Child symbolic gifts by performing anonymous acts of kindness for your Christkindl. The person you are serving is not supposed to know that he or she is your Christkindl, and you are not supposed to know whose Christkindl you have been, until all the identities are revealed on Christmas. By this time, you may have guessed. But it's the thought that counts.

We give to Christ by giving to others without expectation of reward. If we give to Christ in this manner, someday we will be rewarded. This concept has never been easy to understand, and is even harder to understand in an age that worships instant gratification.

SANTA AS SAINT AND SINNER

Santa Claus is omnipresent at Christmas. He's impossible to avoid. His face adorns everything from children's books to advertisements for food and liquor. Wherever you look are icons of Santa, the snowy season's secular saint. Well, Santa is no saint. *But he used to be one.* And therein lies a fascinating but rather sad story.

For ten or eleven centuries, Saint Nicholas was the most popular saint in Christendom. Yet so little is known about the real Nicholas that in 1966 the Catholic Church actually questioned whether he had even existed. There are many legends about Nicholas. The stories change with each telling, but nearly all of them are utterly fantastic. The miracles he allegedly performed include bringing three cannibalized boys back to life. Such stories are clearly the work of folk imagination running wild to fill in the blank spaces of a sketchy biography.

Even the known "facts" have the feeling of embroidery. It is said that Nicholas was born in Asia Minor about 280 CE. He pursued holy orders at a young age and was so quickly elevated to the pastorate that he was known as the "boy bishop." (In those days, a bishop was a parish pastor, not necessarily a supervisor of other pastors.) Nicholas set such a fine example that many pagans were inspired to convert. He was imprisoned during the persecution under Emperor Diocletian, endured many hardships in prison and was freed after five years when the Emperor Constantine legalized Christianity. He returned to his post as Bishop of Myra and served there until his death in 342 or 343 CE.

Nicholas was popularly declared a saint soon after his death. (The process we know as canonization would not be formalized for several more centuries.) Early in the Middle Ages, the day of his death, December 6, became a church feast day, on which people remembered Nicholas' great generosity. They particularly remembered the story of the merchant who had fallen on hard times. The merchant had three daughters and no money to provide a dowry for them. When they came of age and had no suitors, they likely would be sold into prostitution. Hearing of the family's plight, Nicholas secretly delivered three bags of gold to the merchant's home, saving the young women from slavery. It is said that Nicholas threw the bags of gold into the home through an open window or through the smoke hole in the roof, and one of the bags landed in a stocking that had been hung by the fire to dry.

So on the night before Saint Nicholas Day, children began hanging out their stockings or setting their shoes by the fire in hopes that the venerable man's spirit might pass by and fill them with treats. And so he might, if the children had been good. If they hadn't been good, he might leave them a switch, to encourage them to behave better during Advent.

The early Protestant churches wanted nothing to do with a Catholic saint, no matter how popular, so they moved the time of gift giving to Christmas Eve and created Nicholas substitutes. German Protestants favored the notion that the Christ Child himself was the one who delivered the gifts, but they got their images confused. They pictured the Christ Child sometimes as a little angel who wore a crown and sometimes as a girl who wore a garland and candles on her head, the way Saint Lucy did in Italy and Sweden.

One image that endured was that of Father Christmas. Old, pot–bellied, rosy cheeked and usually adorned with flowing white whiskers and a crown of holly, Father Christmas was part benefactor and part rogue. He was equally adept giving presents to children and swilling wine at feasts. And no wonder. He was a reincarnation of several pagan gods, principally the Roman god Saturn, patriarch of the Saturnalia. Saturn himself was a reincarnation of Bacchus, Greek god of wine and lord of the Bacchanalia. The Bacchanalia was a festival of such notorious repute that it was banned by the Romans, who, like us, considered the word "bacchanalia" synonymous with drunken and riotous celebration.

In England, where he found special favor, Father Christmas was gradually tamed to make him fit for children, but he never quite lost his wild edge. The final civilizing took place in America, at the hands of a folklorist, an Episcopal scholar, a political cartoonist, and a commercial artist.

The folklorist was the writer Washington Irving, whose Knickerbocker tales popularized the Dutch tradition of Saint Nicholas and gave it some new twists. For example, Irving's Nicholas flew through the sky on Christmas Eve in a horse-drawn wagon.

The scholar was Clement C. Moore, who in 1822 wrote a poem for his children that he called "A Visit From Saint Nicholas." (Today we more often know it as "The Night Before Christmas.") Moore combined the traits of Saint Nicholas and Father Christmas and the Swedish Christmas gnome known as Jultomten. He created the definitive image of that "right jolly old elf" who flew through the air in a sleigh drawn by eight tiny reindeer.

Political cartoonist Thomas Nast gave the image concrete form in a series of newspaper cartoons from 1863 to 1886. Commerial artist Haddon Sundblom refined the image in a series of Coca-Cola ads from 1931 to 1964.

Even in Moore's time, "Saint Nick" was merely a nickname for Santa Claus. That name is derived from the Dutch "Sinterklaas," which was a childish slurring of Saint Nicholas. The Dutch still preserve the colorful tradition of the saint, and it's easy to see how Santa evolved from him. He also is an old man with a white beard. He wears the long red robes of a bishop and a bishop's tall cap. And he rides a magnificent white horse. Let the beard grow out a little, trim the robes with white fur, flop the cap to one side and replace the horse with reindeer—and you have Santa.

Oh, there are some other changes, too. Nicholas is an Advent figure. Santa does his thing on Christmas Eve. Nicholas talks to children about the importance of preparing for the coming of Jesus. Santa doesn't dare mention Jesus. He might get kicked out of the mall if he did.

THE REALITY OF SANTA

What shall we do with Santa? The old fella obviously means well, but his reputation is pretty tattered these days. Some people know (or at least suspect) that pagan blood flows in his veins and reject him because of his mixed heritage. Others see him as the unwitting villain of a corrupt and socially harmful "Santa Claus theology." Some worry that children will be psychologically damaged when they learn the "truth" about Santa. Others are simply tired of the way he has been taken over by merchandisers.

How you feel about Santa probably stems in large part from your experiences as a child. If Santa was portrayed in your house as a kindly gentleman who loved children and loved to bring them gifts, you'll probably want your own children to regard him with the same warmth. But if your parents harped that "you'd better watch out" or Santa wouldn't bring you anything, you probably think of Santa as an ogre—particularly if, on one or more occasions, he didn't bring you what you wanted.

In other words, you are likely to be the Santa that your parents trained you to be. If you like being that Santa, fine. If you don't, you need to reshape Santa's image.

If you're really down on Santa, you may want to do away with him altogether. Some families have done it, religious families for religious reasons and secular families for secular reasons. If you feel committed to such a course, follow it. But before you set out, carefully consider the consequences. It is not easy to live in this society and not believe in Santa. If you doubt this, ask any of your Jewish friends, who have lifelong experience trying. Santa is a part of our secular culture as well as our religious heritage. He is as much a part of the Christmas season as the Christmas tree and the gifts. If you get rid of him, you will change Christmas radically—perhaps so radically that you destroy the very thing you are trying to preserve.

Santa has been a part of Christmas, in one form or another, for at least a thousand years. A fellow doesn't last that long if he is worthless. There must be some value in his existence, or he would not have endured. The key is discovering that value and conveying it to your children.

Why is Santa such a powerful figure? Perhaps because he embodies a simple and pure truth. Perhaps because if there were no Santa, we would find it necessary to invent one.

Children need fantasy figures. Fact and fantasy live side by side in a child's mind, and fantasy figures can help children sort out which is which as they grow up. Santa is a special fantasy figure. He is like a wise grandparent. He is even, many children will tell you, a lot like God. It's not just that he sees you when you're sleeping, he knows when you're awake and he knows if you've been bad or good. It's what he *does*. He gives unselfishly. He gives without expecting anything in return. Even if you forget to leave milk and cookies for him, he understands.

What he does is *love*.

Where we've gone wrong, lo these many years, is making that love conditional. Those of us who have good childhood memories of Santa felt that he loved us unconditionally. We felt loved as if by a parent or grandparent. We felt loved as if by God.

At his best, Santa symbolizes the spirit of Christmas giving and the spirit of Christian love. And deep down inside, each of us realizes that. So this is one reason we are so upset by the commercialization of Santa. This is why we so fear that children will be traumatized when they learn the "truth" about Santa. Because if love isn't real, life isn't worth living.

IMAGINARY BUT REAL

Each parent must decide how Santa will be explained in each home. It is possible to explain Santa in such a way that he will help children learn to be loving and generous Christians. Here's one way.

First, don't make a big deal out of Santa. Kids will pick up enough of that from their friends and from the constant exposure to Santa in the media and at the shopping centers. Don't discourage belief in Santa, just gently downplay his significance. If you have a few favorite Santa objects among your Christmas decorations, keep them. But don't plaster your walls with Santa icons. Keep Santa as a part of your Christmas, but don't give him top billing. And if you display images of Saint Nicholas rather than Santa, so much the better.

Second, treat Santa as a fairy tale figure. Make it clear to your children from their earliest days that Santa is imaginary. This is not to say that Santa is not *real*. Santa is very real. He just isn't real in that same way that you and I are real. He is as real as any other of your children's storybook characters. He is as real as Benjamin Bunny. He is as real as that Velveteen Rabbit who discovered that he could become real by learning to love.

So what about all those men in the red suits you see on television and at the mall? They're not the real Santa. Those are all Santa's *helpers*. Santa has many helpers. Among them are moms and dads and grandparents and friends and brothers and sisters. We're *all* Santa's helpers, because what Santa does is love other people and show his love by giving them presents, and we do that, too.

Christmas presents don't just fall from the sky. They have to be given by someone. Santa gives presents. So do we all. So we are all Santas in our own way. Mom and Dad are Santa Claus. So are Grandma and Grandpa. So are Uncle Dick and Aunt Jan. So is big brother and little sister. We're all Santa Claus because Santa lives in each of us.

This is getting close to theology, isn't it? That's precisely the point. Santa is a fantasy figure, but he points to a reality that children aren't yet ready to understand. He's a bridge to understanding. If we treat Santa in the right way, if we don't try to make him real in the wrong way, children won't be gravely disappointed when they learn the "truth" about Santa. It will slowly dawn on them that Santa is only as real as love itself.

As your children grow, explain that although Santa is imaginary, he is based on a real person who was called Saint Nicholas. Nicholas lived a long time ago, and then he died. But he set such a fine example during his life that he has come to represent the spirit of giving itself. He can't give any more, so he depends on us to follow his example of giving. If anyone is to receive a present at Christmas, one of us will have to give it in Santa's name.

This explanation is a subtle lesson in the foundation of Christian theology. Jesus also lived a long time ago, and he also died. God raised Jesus from the dead, but then Jesus went back to live with God. Jesus can live within us today, too, if we allow him. And Jesus depends on us to live the way he did, to live *for* him. Jesus doesn't have a body any more. We are his body now. We are the visible body of the invisible Christ, and whatever we do for others we do in his stead.

You may think this farfetched. You may be offended by the notion that belief in Santa can help foster belief in Jesus. You may think that we're reading Jesus into Santa in an effort to justify Santa and are treading near blasphemy. But think about it. Who came first? Saint Nicholas or Jesus? Why was Saint Nicholas so beloved? Because he tried to be like Jesus. Because Jesus lived in him.

You may have heard it said: "Your life may be the only Bible some people ever read. You may be the only Jesus they ever meet." If Jesus doesn't live in us, he is no more real to us than Santa Claus. Can I put it any more baldly? Try this: If we don't make Santa a Christ figure, he will become a satanic figure.

The theology behind Santa is vital. Because if we don't interpret Santa in Christian terms, our children will interpret Santa in secular terms. We are absolutely right in rejecting the secular Santa. He *is* an ogre. Jesus does not live in him; Satan does.

What does the secular Santa preach? That he is like God. That he sees all and knows all and judges all. Judgment day comes once a year, on Christmas. Christmas is when the secular Santa rewards good boys and girls and punishes bad girls and boys. If you're good, you get a reward. If you're bad, you get nothing. If your family has money, you're good. If you're poor, you're bad.

This is not the message of Jesus, who came to preach "good news to the poor" (Luke 4:18). This is the message of Satan, who preaches bad news to the poor and worse news to the rich.

It follows, then, that you must never use Christmas gifts as a bribe to your children. Not *ever*. Teach them that a gift is a sign of love. Teach them that they receive gifts not because they are good or bad but because they are loved. Guide their expectations. Don't let them dream of gifts that are too beautiful to be possible. Make "wish lists" and go over them carefully and lovingly. Make your children understand that the size of the gifts they receive has nothing to do with the size of your love for them. It has only to do with how much money you can afford (or want to afford) to spend on gifts. And how much money you have in your wallet has nothing to do with how much love you have in your heart.

Tell them that many other children are not as privileged as they are. Tell them that many other children will awaken on Christmas morning and find very small gifts, or no gifts at all, waiting for them. Tell them that this is very sad. But your family can help make it less sad. Your family can help these poor children. You can be like Saint Nicholas. You can be a Santa to these children. You can help them feel loved. By giving to them. By loving them. Anonymously. Without expectation of return.

What does a child want from Christmas? A new doll, a new train set—the same things a child always wants when presented with such possibilities. What does a child want on Christmas? The same things that any adult always wants—the security of being loved.

Christmas is about love. We don't have to complicate it.

I remember the Christmas right after our older daughter, Jennifer, turned two. We lived in northern Michigan at the time, and we traveled to central Kansas to visit Linda's parents for the holidays. Jennifer was the first grandchild on that side of the family. We lived so far away that no one got to see her very often, so everyone gave her excessive numbers of gifts. Sitting on the floor in front of the Christmas tree, surrounded by more packages than she could imagine and exhausted by opening one after another, she shrieked, "Too many presents!"

We all looked at one another nervously and smiled at her childish objection. But we knew she was right.

Christmas is about love. We don't have to complicate it.

Chapter Six

The December Dilemma

A friend who is Jewish recalls that when she was a child, she was always envious of her Christian friends at Christmas because Santa Claus never came to her house. When she was grown and married, she and her husband put up a tree and celebrated Christmas for their first few years together, lavishing gifts on each other to make up for the losses of Christmases past. Then they stopped. Although they might give each other a small present now and again, they've gotten Santa out of their systems. Santa doesn't matter to them anymore.

If you want to look at Christmas from a new perspective, consider the millions of people in this country who don't celebrate Christmas. These include Jews, Muslims, Buddhists, Hindus and, in the Christian camp, Jehovah's Witnesses. For these people and others, including many atheists, the coming of winter poses what has become known as "the December dilemma." Simply put, it is, "What shall we do about Christmas?"

How do these parents respond when their children come home from day care with crayon–colored drawings of Santa and ask, "Why doesn't Santa come to our house?"

It's a cruel question. And it's not enough to answer, "We don't celebrate Christmas in our house," for children of all cultural backgrounds respond instinctively to Santa and the hope of presents. To meet the expectations of our culture, many people of diverse faiths *do* exchange gifts at Christmas. But many of them are uncomfortable with the idea.

Christmas is the only religious holy day that is a legal holiday throughout the United States. It may be easy to avoid the sacred Christmas in America, but escaping the secular Christmas is nearly impossible. Even the secular Christmas has enough religious associations (if only historical ones) that devout adherents of other faiths, and strict atheists as well, regard it cautiously.

Some Hindus and others find their faith open enough to encompass a religious celebration of Christmas. People of most other faith traditions don't have such flexibility. Muslims consider Jesus a great prophet but don't celebrate his birthday, or any other. Jehovah's Witnesses don't celebrate birthdays either. People of some other religions and cultures can rely on their own winter holidays. Buddhists have the Chinese New Year. Jews have Hanukkah.

Hanukkah has been stereotyped among Gentiles as "the Jewish Christmas." It's true that some Jews have felt pressured to Christianize—or perhaps more precisely, to "Christmas-ize"—Hanukkah. At one extreme, this involves putting up a tree and calling it a "Hanukkah bush." A more common concession is the giving of small presents on several or all of the eight days of the festival. Just as Christmas could not escape some trappings of the winter season, so has Hanukkah absorbed some winter solstice customs.

The Christmas and Hanukkah seasons share several similarities. Both fall in December. Both tell the story of a miracle, and both use images of light. Hanukkah is a minor festival in the Jewish religious calendar, but it may have something to tell us about the future of Christmas.

The Feast of Dedication, or Feast of Lights, as it also is known, celebrates a successful rebellion against Syrian rule of Israel and the rededication of the Temple in Jerusalem in 165 BCE. The Syrian king, Antiochus Epiphanes, had tried to destroy Judaism and force Hellenistic culture on the Jews. Antiochus forbade the worship of God and set up idols in the Temple. When Jewish rebels led by Judas Maccabee threw off Syrian control, they sought to purify the Temple and restore the worship of God.

However, when they went to rekindle the Eternal Light that burned in the Temple, the Maccabees found only enough consecrated olive oil to last for one day. Miraculously, the lamp burned for eight days, until new oil could be properly consecrated. To commemorate this miracle, Jewish families light one new candle each evening during Hanukkah until, on the final evening, all eight candles of the menorah are burning.

Hanukkah is a joyous celebration, filled with games, songs and, yes, gifts. One of the things it celebrates is religious freedom. And one of the principles it teaches is that of religious tolerance. That is why it is ironic that Christmas customs are rubbing off on Hanukkah. *One of the things Hanukkah celebrates is the right to be different.*

It is a right that is becoming increasingly important in America. However "Christian" the United States ever was, in any meaningful sense, it is becoming more religiously pluralistic. Some Christians view this trend with suspicion and even alarm because their beliefs and sensibilities often seem to fall victim to it. They are used to being top dog, and they resent not being treated that way. Nevertheless, if ours is indeed a free country, all of our people must be free to worship as they wish. And no religion has the right to force its traditions on another.

The implications of this trend for Christmas have become obvious. Our society is growing in its cultural diversity. But Christmas is not a pluralistic holiday. It is, fundamentally, a Christian holiday. The trend toward pluralism means that the secular Christmas will keep trying to edge the sacred Christmas out of the picture. The season will become even more secularized as Jesus becomes more marginalized.

As Christians, we may say that Jesus is the reason for the season. But public policy is pushing Jesus to the margins of our society, and the secular Christmas has assumed center place in law as well as practice.

THE NEW FREEDOM OF RELIGION

By the time our younger daughter got to the public elementary school, there were no Nativity scenes displayed at school in December. There were no pictures of angels or Wise Men, and certainly no images of baby Jesus. There were only drawings of snowmen and reindeer and, of course, Santa Claus.

If Erica had taken a Nativity scene for sharing time, she would be allowed to tell what it meant to her and answer questions from her classmates. If Erica had wanted to draw a picture of baby Jesus for art class, she would have been free to do it. But the school could not *require* her to color a picture of baby Jesus. And to avoid even the possibility of coercion, the school would not even give her the option. Her teacher would never have handed her a picture of baby Jesus and say, "You can color this if you wish, but you don't *have* to," because the very act of *handing* her the picture might imply coercion.

Welcome to freedom of religion in the American public schools. You may not like it a lot. But you need to understand it, and understanding it means going beyond the politically correct "They've taken religion out of our schools!" clichés that so many people resort to in these debates.

Freedom of religion is a sacred principle to Americans. But we may never all agree about *how* the principle should be applied in daily life. Perhaps nowhere is the fight more heated than in the public schools, which are always near the front lines of our culture wars.

On the one hand are those who argue that expressions of religion must not be encouraged in schools because inevitably such expressions imply government sanction and coercion. Simply put, if the teacher hands out pictures of baby Jesus for pupils to color, the teacher is supporting the Christian observance of Christmas and coercing students to comply with it.

On the other hand are those who argue that discouraging expressions of religion in the schools actively encourages another world view, a "secular religion" that has no right to be sanctioned and coerced by government. If the teacher fails to provide even the option of coloring a baby Jesus, the teacher is supporting a secular observance of Christmas and coercing students to comply with it.

Starkly put, it's a battle between sacred and the secular Christmases, and there is no safe middle ground. In a reasonable world, perhaps we could come to terms with one another and forge a compromise that we could all live with. But this is not a reasonable world, and we are not always dealing with reasonable people.

Let's say that at the beginning of the school year all the parents get together with all the teachers and the principal and decide that the school is going to support the cultural diversity of the community by affirming and celebrating all the religious and cultural traditions that are represented. This means that there'll be pictures of baby Jesus at Christmas, a menorah at Hanukkah and paper lanterns for the Chinese New Year. There also will be events to mark Muslim and Hindu holy days and special presentations to acquaint the children with customs of Jehovah's Witnesses and other religious groups. No student will be under any compulsion to participate in any celebratory event, but, in the spirit of *education*, each student will be required to learn something about all the traditions. Those students who have no religious tradition will not be required to participate in any celebratory event, but, like all the other students, they will be exposed to the religious traditions of all the others. And, yes, atheism or some other form of secularism also could be represented.

Sound reasonable? Think we could work this out? Not on your life!

A parent who is an atheist will complain that because her child is being forced to learn about the existence of religion, the child actually is being *taught* religion. A parent who is a Muslim fundamentalist or a Christian fundamentalist will complain that his child is being subjected to the Satanic practices of heathens and other secularists. The whole experiment will come crashing down because of the objections of just a few people.

People with extreme views tend to be the ones who push the hardest and file the lawsuits that set the precedents that govern public policy. One atheist who insists that freedom of religion means freedom from *exposure* to religion can doom almost any effort to include religious expression in schools. One fundamentalist who insists that freedom of religion means freedom from all *other* religious thought can thwart the most well-intentioned efforts to include a diversity of religious expression in schools.

This situation will continue until Congress or the Supreme Court sets a workable standard that guarantees full expression of religious diversity in the schools without stepping on the rights of those who object to religion or diversity. If I knew how to draft such a standard, I would have sent a copy to my senators or representatives a long time ago. If you know how to draft such a law, please send a copy to Washington immediately. Until such a measure is enacted, there may be no genuine freedom of religion in American schools, only an uneasy truce in our increasingly strident culture wars.

RIGHTS AND WRONGS

In the small Illinois town where I spent some of my formative years, there is a small city park where a Nativity scene used to be erected every December. I have not checked lately, but I am sure that the little wooden crib and shelter can be found in that park no longer. It is city property, which some critics say is not a proper place for a public display of religion.

Many communities have fought long and bitter legal battles over their Nativity scenes, city seals that mention a deity and other public symbols. Seeing what has happened to those in the "vanguard" of social change, other communities simply cave in at the first sign of a fight because they are fearful of the legal expense and the likelihood that, no matter how much they pay their lawyers, they will lose—and even if they "win," it will feel a lot like losing.

Minor victories do occur. In Cincinnati some years ago, a Jewish group used a freedom of religion argument to win the right to display a menorah in a public park. The Ku Klux Klan promptly went to court and used the same argument to win the right to erect a cross in the same park. The Klan said its cross was a Christian symbol. (It's not the biggest lie ever argued in court, but it may be among the top 10. Genuine Christianity does not promote hate.)

Such ironies mount as the battle intensifies over the role of religion in public life. The situation is touchiest in the schools, which are extremely sensitive to political pressure from all quarters. School principals like to avoid trouble at all cost. If there is a chance that allowing a religious display will bring a lawsuit, they will lean toward not allowing the religious display, *even if a ban on religious displays is not required by any reasonable interpretation of the law.* The guiding principle, I've been told, is to keep your head down and keep your name out of the news.

Some Christians have gotten to be just as fond of filing suits as atheists have been, so school principals often find themselves in a lose–lose situation. The American Center for Law and Justice was founded by religious broadcaster Pat Robertson to pursue such legal efforts. It also works to make sure that government officials know the rules of religious speech and don't always lean the other way in interpreting them.

The ACLJ says one reason it exists is to counter activities of the American Civil Liberties Union, which has filed or supported many of the suits that have resulted in limits on some religious expressions in public life. The ACLU says the goals of the groups are not in conflict; both seek to safeguard freedom of religion. But many Christians see the ACLU as an enemy because its actions appear to have helped create a legal climate in which the freedoms of some are shrunk and the freedoms of others are inflated.

Many religious people of all faiths now feel under attack by their own government. They think the judicial system is destroying religious life by trying so hard to protect the freedom of those who are hostile to religion. And they may be right, though not necessarily in the way they think they are right.

The fight over Nativity scenes is instructive. Court interpretations have varied, but they seem to tend toward allowing Nativity scenes in public places if they are part of a display that has a secular theme overall. In other words, a religious display is permitted if it is overwhelmed by the secular display or is so innocuous that it is virtually inconspicuous. A religious display is permitted if it is secularized or marginalized. Jesus is acceptable as long as he is irrelevant!

FREEDOM THROUGH DIVERSITY

If Jesus is not the reason for the season, who or what is? Listen to the sounds of cash registers, and you will understand. The mercantile Christmas, unhindered by a single religious thought, is about all that's left.

Can you see the way history could be moving here? Two or three centuries after Jesus' death, Christians in Rome decide to celebrate his birthday during the traditionally rowdy winter solstice season. The new holy day picks up many of the solstice customs and the partying gets so out of hand that some Christians try to stamp out the holy day as well as the customs. This all-out attack breaks the fragile link between holy day and popular custom, so the two now pursue separate courses and influence each other only from a distance. Then activists seeking greater freedom of religion pursue policies that actually are hostile to religion, making the holy day appear irrelevant apart from the holiday that has grown up around it. Finally there may come the time when Christmas is a sort of a glorified Ground Hog Day—and hardly anybody can quite remember how either quaint tradition got started.

It doesn't have to end that way. But it could if we don't redefine our Christmas celebration in a way that witnesses strongly to the integrity of our faith. We have to demonstrate to society that Christmas without Christ is a hollow shell.

Like the gospel itself, this is a message many people are not disposed to hear. Some people are perfectly happy with the secular Christmas. They don't want Christ in Christmas, and they resent our efforts to keep him there. "Can't you keep your religion out of it?" they grouse. Others are aware of the spiritual bankruptcy of the secular Christmas and celebrate it as little as possible—but they, too, see Christian efforts to revitalize the holiday as an intrusion into their lives. "Look," they say, "if Christmas is what your religion represents, I don't want any part of it."

Note that both attitudes represent the school of thought that interprets freedom of religion as freedom *from* religion. We have to respect that line of thought because it would be wrong to try to force our beliefs on others. But we have to combat such thinking as well, by claiming our own freedom and our own rights. We have to remember the lesson of Hanukkah. *Others have a right to be different. So do we.*

If we are to assert our rights, we cannot do it on the basis of exclusivity. We must do it on the basis of diversity. That's the only way we'll retain our rights legally, and it's the only way we can retain them morally. We're not asking much. We're asking no more than Ebenezer Scrooge asked of his nephew, Fred, when he said: "Nephew, you keep Christmas in your way, and let me keep it in mine."

Freedom *means* diversity. So perhaps the Nativity scene will have to share the city park with a Santa and a menorah and maybe even a vile Klan cross. Perhaps we have to share the park in the same way that we share our community and our country. Perhaps in this diversity we can see the hope of our faith flourishing not because it is culturally dominant but because it offers a message that people need and want to hear.

IT'S A WAR OUT THERE

Every once in a while, some Christmas tree salesman puts up a sign on his lot advertising "XMAS TREES." Soon the ranks of the easily offended swell with indignation, and the tree lot becomes the focus of some preacher's Outrage of the Week Club. "It's time to put Christ back into Christmas!" the preacher thunders, and the faithful cheer and vow to boycott the lot and its godless trees.

It's all based on misunderstanding and ignorance—misunderstanding on the part of the faithful masses and ignorance (often willful) on the part of any preacher who's involved. In ancient Greek, the language of the New Testament, "X" is the first letter of the name "Christ." For nearly twenty centuries, "X" has been a shorthand way of referring to Jesus. "X" was widely recognized as the sign of the Christ until only recently. Now ignorance of classical languages and classical usage is so widespread that most people think "X" must refer to "Brand X" or maybe the "The X-Files." Therefore, using "X" in place of "Christ" must be an attempt to "X" Christ right out of Christmas.

Well, the tree salesman may have chosen "XMAS" because it lines up rather neatly with the word "TREES" on a sign.

XMAS
TREES

Or maybe he thought that following a 2,000-year-old custom might be a way of honoring the one whose name the trees represent. Either way, he probably is not a card-carrying member of that Vast Conspiracy to Stamp Out Christmas As We Know It. That conspiracy is mostly a fiction.

It's a gimmick designed to further someone's political agenda or boost their political clout.

Bill O'Reilly called his TV show a "no-spin zone," but spin is all it ever was. If the host's favorite description of his show is a whopper, what should that tell you about the show itself? For several years, O'Reilly waged a noisy campaign against the "war on Christmas." He claimed that "secular progressives" were out to destroy traditional American values and that Christmas was the beachhead of their assault. A frequent cohort in this campaign was Fox Network broadcaster John Gibson, author of a political screed titled *The War on Christmas: How the Liberal Plot to Ban the Sacred Holiday Is Worse Than You Thought.*

Several self-described "conservative" Christian groups have gotten into the act. They sell pro-Christmas paraphernalia to counter the anti-Christmas campaign they see everywhere. "It's just a fund-raising scam," their critics say.[53] The situation does seem reminiscent of those "action alerts" that used to appear regularly warning of new assaults on religion from atheist crusader Madalyn Murray O'Hair, even long after she was dead. Most of those alerts turned out to be fiction, too.

Footnote: Donald Trump congratulated himself several times in 2017 and 2018 for "saving Christmas," and several of his sycophants noisily echoed that claim. As usual, his bluster was devoid of factual basis—if only because Bill O'Reilly had already claimed that *he* saved Christmas in 2014. The whole "war on Christmas" schtick is part of an elaborate right-wing fantasy that can be traced to the John Birch Society in 1959, and before that to Henry Ford, who claimed that Jews were trying to destroy both Christmas and Easter.[54] In 2018, progressive Christian blogger John Pavlovitz declared that there was, indeed, a war on Christmas—and it was being waged by white evangelicals against the real meaning of Christsmas. He took a similar, though slightly less strident, tone in a column two years earlier, when he said there was *no war* on Christmas.[55]

Despite its slippery underpinnings, the notion that Christmas is under attack has great resonance with people. The movie "Last Ounce of Freedom" was filmed in Paola, the small Kansas town where I once served as pastor of the local United Methodist Church. Some scenes were staged just down the street from the church. One cold night, we opened the fellowship hall to the cast and crew so they would have a place to eat and stay warm between scenes being shot outdoors.

Publicity for the movie announced: "Our freedoms are under attack. Christmas is next." I think the whole notion is poppycock. What *is* under attack is the freedom of one set of people to impose their version of Christmas on others. What *is* under attack is the freedom of some people to limit the freedom of others.

So-called "conservatives" aren't the only ones playing this game. The Freedom From Religion Foundation, which fancies itself a coalition of freethinkers, has an annoying habit of demanding that its winter solstice sign be placed in public places alongside Nativity scenes and other such displays.

The sign says: "At this season of the Winter Solstice, may reason prevail. There are no gods, no devils, no angels, no heaven or hell. There is only our natural world. Religion is but myth and superstition that hardens hearts and enslaves minds."

The language is deliberately provocative. A "freethinking" spokesperson explains: "Once a government declares a public forum for religion, the only way to fight back is to place a sign that causes as much discomfort to believers as a nativity display . . . causes nonbelievers, as well as those of us who cherish the constitutional separation between church and state."

Well, a lot of us who cherish the separation of church and state think that the sign is offensive and stupid. But being offensive and stupid is apparently part of the game our society must play every year at Christmas as we battle over the proper role of sacred and secular in the public square.

SO LONG, CHRISTENDOM

A group that calls itself the Christian Anti-Defamation Commission says that its mission is to "advance religious liberty for Christians." Note the exclusive focus. If you're not Christian, look out. The group's web site ticks off the latest assaults on Christian America and has offered such sidebars as "Seven Reasons Barack Obama is not a Christian." See, it's not enough to claim Jesus as your Savior and Lord. You have to do it *their way*. So the group is even more exclusive. It exists to advance religious liberty only for *some* Christians.

Gary Case, the group's leader, says Christian values ought to rule in America because America is a Christian nation. "We are the majority," he says. Bowing to pressure from others leads to the "tyranny of the minority."

Let's set aside, for the moment, the debate over whether America is or ever was or ever could be in any biblical sense a "Christian nation." Instead, let's debate whether America is a *free* nation. A free nation protects the freedom of all its citizens and grants special freedoms to none. A majority rule that fails to protect the rights of minorities is a tyranny. Tyranny is tyranny whether it is enforced by a minority or by a majority. If America is free for Christians only, it is not a free nation. If America is free for one religion only, then America is no more free than Iran or North Korea or any other tyranny you can name.

What "social conservatives" decry is not the *death* of freedom but the *birth* of freedom. What they attack is not a limitation of their freedom but an end to their privilege to limit the freedoms of others. When they bemoan the death of "freedom as we know it," what they are really bemoaning is the death of Christendom.

Christendom is the identification of Christianity with the state. The Roman Emperor Constantine is usually credited (or blamed) with the creation of Christendom. Constantine pointed the direction, but it was actually one of his successors, Theodosius I, who abolished pagan worship and made Christianity the established religion of the Roman Empire.

As the church quickly learned, being an established religion presents certain intractable problems:

- Everyone is presumed to be Christian, even if they aren't really.
- Christianity becomes an increasingly superficial civil religion.
- Religion becomes identified with existing social norms.
- God exists primarily to support the prevailing power structure.
- Religious dissent equals political dissent, and both must be eradicated.
- If church equals culture, the religious inevitably becomes secularized.
- Church may have the form of religion, but its heart is elsewhere.
- Established religion, in short, leads to the death of real religion.

Despite these and other problems, Christendom was the dominant cultural paradigm in Western Civilization for more than a thousand years. The edifice started to crack during the Protestant Reformation, when national churches assumed the spiritual authority that had been held up to that time by the pope alone. The big Roman Catholic Christendom was shattered into many little Christendoms.

Christendom was the norm in several of the American colonies. To be a citizen of the colony, you had to be a member of the established church. Several colonies were founded by people who fled their homelands because they dissented from the particular brand of Christendom that was established there. In their new homes, they created their own Christendoms and persecuted *others* who dissented.

When the United States was created, the authors of the Constitution remembered the religious wars that had savaged Europe for centuries not so long before, and they rejected the establishment of any church as the official religion of the land. However, by that time several Protestant churches were so firmly established *culturally* that they didn't have to be established *politically*. For nearly two centuries, Protestant churches enjoyed cultural supremacy and religious dominance. The entire social order supported Protestant belief, promoted it and rewarded it. The schools taught religion and prayer because it was thought that such things made good citizens. But even the uneducated picked up the basics of religion by osmosis because Protestant Christian symbolism was everywhere.

It is this cultural supremacy that many people are referring to when they say that America is a "Christian nation." America has in many ways always been Christian culturally—that is, superficially. Flag and country and Bible have gotten all mixed up in a civil religion that is very easy to accept because it requires so little of anybody except obedience to the norm. But where is the demanding gospel of Jesus? Where is the love of God revealed in the love of the neighbor and the alien?

It's easy being Christian under Christendom. You don't have to do much more than just show up. It's easy being the church under Christendom. The culture props you up and does half your work for you. But what happens when Christendom starts to crumble and the prop fails? Suddenly you're not the top dog anymore. You're just one religion among many. You can't make others do what you want because the culture has revoked your authority to throw your weight around. Now you're back in the world that Christians inhabited for the first three hundred years after Jesus died. Now you've got to go back to being *in* the world but not *of* it.

What we are seeing in much of our culture wars is the angry reaction of people who want Christendom restored. These people are mad because they don't have the power they think they should have. But Christendom is dying—and "liberals" aren't killing it. Atheists and secularists aren't killing it either. Christendom is dying because of its own inner contradictions.

Christendom is dying because when Christ equals culture, Christ becomes an unnecessary accessory. Christendom always eventually produces secular societies. What has happened in America is that American culture has changed so that it no longer supports a superficial civil religion that passes for biblical Christianity.

We may legitimately mourn the passing of "the good old days," when just about everybody knew some Bible stories. But we ought to acknowledge that knowing these stories was never enough. Knowing these stories did not produce fully committed Christians. It is *good* that Christendom is dying. Now we can jettison the shallow religion of Christendom and replace it with the fully engaging gospel of Jesus Christ. The passing of Christendom presents us with an unprecedented opportunity to preach the truth to the world—and maybe, because we are no longer identified with oppressive social structures, some people who desperately need to hear the message will finally be able and willing to hear it.

SO LONG, "CHRISTIAN AMERICA"

America's founders could have created a nation with an established religion. They could have forged a United States that was consciously Christian. But they declined to do so. The Constitution doesn't mention God or Christ. The First Amendment to the Constitution says: "Congress shall make no law respecting an establishment of religion, or prohibiting the free exercise thereof..."

Notice what these two clauses *do*. They prohibit state–established religion. They prohibit limitations on the free exercise of religion.

Notice what these two clauses do *not* do. They do not create a "Christian America." A Christian America is an establishment of religion and therefore is prohibited by the Constitution. These two clauses *also* do not create a "godless America." They do not remove the expression of religion from the public square.

What the founders clearly believed is that:

1. Religion belongs in the public square.
2. One form of religion cannot be allowed to exercise exclusive influence in the public square by excluding others.

The founders separated church and state but did not remove religion from the political arena. Far from it! They created a system that guaranteed that we would be fighting about it for as long as the Republic exists.

Any establishment of religion is, by definition, a limitation on the free exercise of religion. Whenever one religion is officially or unofficially sanctioned by the state, it receives special support from the state that other religions do not receive. It enjoys special privilege in the society.

Despite the First Amendment, churches representing certain forms of Christianity have historically enjoyed special privilege in this country. Some of these churches are now crying foul because this privilege is eroding. It is eroding because America is learning, after more than 200 years, that an establishment of religion does not have to be formal to do harm to religious freedom. Even if an establishment of religion is informal and socially acceptable, it still endangers freedom.

Newsweek magazine caused a stir with its April 13, 2009 cover story announcing "The Decline and Fall of Christian America." It looked like one of those skeptical stories that news magazines typically produced right before Easter while the umpteenth rerun of "The Ten Commandments" was playing on television. But the story turned out to be a sober assessment of important demographic changes in the religious landscape of America.

The cover headline overstates the case the story is trying to make. What the story describes is "the decline and fall of the religious right's notion of a Christian America." Although author Jon Meacham never mentions the word "Christendom," that is clearly part of what he is thinking about. "The End of Christian America" is the end of America's Christendom, that informal and socially acceptable civil religion that has prevailed for most of our history.

Meacham, who was then the managing editor of *Newsweek*, also is author of the book *American Gospel: The Founding Fathers and the Making of a Nation*. In that book, Meacham argues that the founders were careful not to support any form of sectarian religion. Rather, they chose to support what Benjamin Franklin called "public religion," invoking a generic, non-sectarian God. This "public religion" is apparently what President Dwight D. Eisenhower famously endorsed when he said: "Our form of government makes no sense unless it is founded in a deeply felt religious faith, and I don't care what it is."[56]

One form of this "public religion" is represented by America's mainline churches, which in the last 50 years became so identified with the culture that they rendered themselves irrelevant. Now the "conservative" forms of American civil religion are suffering a similar erosion of influence. Dying with them is their dream of "Christian America." Like the Victorian re-creation of Christmas, it is a nostalgic invention with only tenuous links to the past.

When talking about "Christian America," we need to draw several important distinctions. The chief distinction is the difference between being a nation of Christians and being a Christian nation. No one denies that a majority of Americans call themselves Christian, or that Christian belief plays a major role in shaping national policy. But that does not mean that America is, or ever has been, or ever could be, in any real sense a Christian nation.

President Obama was harshly criticized by some when he declared in 2009 that America is not a Christian nation. He was not the first president to say that. The first president to say it was George Washington. The whole notion ought to be upsetting to any thinking Christian. To call this, or any other, nation "Christian" is to so cheapen the commands of Jesus that it runs perilously close to blasphemy. The idea of a Christian nation belongs in the trash heap along with the heresy that spawned it—the heresy called Christendom.

Identification of church with state is almost always disastrous for the church. When church and state come together, guess which one loses its identity? The horrors of the Crusades and the Inquisition and centuries of European religious wars are the natural outcome of such confused thinking. Such outcomes are natural because the whole notion of Christendom is a terrible theological mistake.

Biblical Christianity knows nothing of Christendom. Search the New Testament diligently and you will find many references to the church being the object of persecution by the state. You will find nothing about the church ruling *as* the state or *with* the state. The church of the New Testament was a minority marked for persecution. The church is victorious only in its perseverance in time of trial. The final victory is God's, when the reign of God that Jesus inaugurated is fully revealed. But the church is not the kingdom of God, and neither is the state, whether the state is secular or religious.

God's plan is not to create a political entity. "My kingdom is not from this world," Jesus said (John 18:36). God's plan is not the takeover of the world by coercion but by love. God's plan is not to force people to behave but one by one to transform people into loving imitations of Jesus.

Our job as Christians is not to make America a Christian nation, but to make America a nation of Christians. We have done a poor job of it. That is one reason—maybe the biggest reason—that our influence is declining. Mainliners have pretty much abdicated their voice, and the loud voices of intolerance from the so-called "evangelical" wing are growing increasingly tiresome. We need to discover an authentic Christian voice to re-engage our world—and, not incidentally, to save the soul of Christmas.

CLOTHING THE PUBLIC SQUARE

In an important book in 1984, Richard John Neuhaus warned against the dangers of a "Naked Public Square." This is a public space that is shorn of all religious dialogue. It is a space where secular attitudes prevail and religious attitudes are constantly pushed to the margins until, oops, they fall off the map entirely. [57]

State-sponsored secularism is no less an establishment of religion than a state-sponsored church. The public square cannot be naked. It will be clothed in *something*. The "freethinkers" who want religious discourse banned because it is "superstition" simply want to promote their own forms of superstition. Christendom is not the only tyranny that wants to play by special rules that give it an advantage.

Religious discourse cannot be banned from the public square. Nor can it be given special privilege. What we need, as Neuhaus has said many times, is not a *naked* public square but a *civil* public square.

The establishment and free exercise provisions of the U.S. Constitution are two sides of the same coin. But some judges keep trying to set the provisions against each other and do away with all religious arguments, thus nullifying both provisions.

It is deeply ironic that both state-sponsored secularism and state-sponsored religion lead to the death of religion—and the death of freedom as well. The state exists to preserve freedom, not limit it. Therefore, the state must assure that no form of belief (or unbelief) becomes established by law or by custom.

So Baby Jesus may have to share the public square not only with Santa and Frosty the Snowman but also with the Buddha and even with obnoxious solstice celebrants. It would be simpler if those on the fringes would just let everybody else be, but that's not likely to happen. So the war over Christmas will go on. It *has* to go on, because this tension is at the heart of what it means to be an American who lives free and wants all his or her brothers and sisters to live free as well—even those who abuse their freedom, even those who don't have the faintest idea what freedom really means, even those who want to take away some of your freedom so they will have more for themselves.

SKIPPING CHRISTMAS (OR, "NEVER ON SUNDAY")

It happened in 1994 and 2005 and 2011 and 2016, and it will happen next in 2022. The pattern is regular, but the occurrence is just infrequent enough that we tend to forget about it. Every four, six or 11 years, Christmas falls on a Sunday. Talk about a December dilemma!

Sunday is the normal day of worship for most Christians, so you might think that Christmas falling on a Sunday would be a happy coincidence—one to celebrate. Not so in modern America. In 2005, while Bill O'Reilly and others were battling to put their partisan Christ "back" into Christmas, several megachurches decided to skip Christmas altogether. They had stayed open in 1994, when Christmas also fell on a Sunday, and attendance was light. Their members had voted with their feet, and the churches capitulated to the will of the majority. The sacred Christmas lost. The winner was the domestic Christmas, a subset of the secular/consumer Christmas. Rather than gathering with other believers to worship as the church, the way Christians normally might on any given Sunday, people stayed home to worship at the altar of family and gifts.

For the record: I am a retired United Methodist pastor who still serves a church part-time. In 2005 and 2012 and 2016, my churches were open for worship. Attendance was lower than normal, just about what you might expect for any major holiday weekend. But we had a great time. Maybe that's the way Christmas *ought* to be done. Still, I suspect that more people might rebel if we tried to have church on December 25 *every* year, especially those years when it *doesn't* fall on a Sunday.

I am aware that I am one who has not celebrated a "normal" Christmas in many years. For my family, Christmas Eve has always involved one or two candlelight worship services. Traveling to Grandma's house has long been out of the question because Daddy had to "work." Now both Linda and I are pastoring churches—*different* churches, of course—so if we travel at all around Christmas, we must do it late on Christmas Eve or on Christmas or the day after. But most families are not trained this way. They are used to more freedom, and so they are more likely to resent the idea that churches might want to be open on the biggest family day of the year.

I also am aware that, historically, Christmas grew the most in popularity after it was domesticated. Christmas became the cultural force it is only when its primary celebration was moved from the public arena to the home hearth. Churches jumped on the Christmas bandwagon relatively late in the game, and they're still riding the culture's coattails. When we try to make people feel guilty about skipping church when Christmas falls on Sunday, we are introducing a new concept. We are trying to convert people to the sacred Christmas when their primary allegiance is still to the cultural/secular/domestic Christmas.

It's another sign of what a poor job we have done at winning people to Christ. Christian nation, indeed! You can't even get people to church on Christmas! If Christmas is the big religious deal we make it out to be, why *wouldn't* people want to be in church then?

KEEPING CHRISTMAS

Non-Christians aren't the only ones who face "the December dilemma." Christians also must ask themselves, "What shall we do about Christmas?"

Before you can answer that question for yourself, you need to decide what Christmas means to you and what you want out of it. Then you'll know what to do about it, and you'll know how to keep it.

Everyone wants a joyous Christmas, but people disagree on what makes Christmas joyful. If you want a joyous Christmas, you have to invent it for yourself.

Many others, certainly, will go a different way. Let them go in peace, and wish them well. Let them keep Christmas their way as you keep it your way. That's called freedom.

How *shall* you keep Christmas? That's the subject of our final chapter.

Chapter Seven

A Blessed Christmas

Christmas can be the best of times or the worst of times. Christmas is what we make of it. We *can* celebrate Christmas better than we do. If we call ourselves Christians, we must. The challenge of Christmas is the challenge of life itself. We need to embrace it fully and glorify God in and through it.

In previous chapters, I have dropped hints on how I think this can be done. The time has come to repeat some of these suggestions in a more systematic way. If you follow them, you may be able to make your next Christmas the kind of blessed event you've always known it could be.

This is a rough summation of my own spiritual and intellectual journey toward an understanding of Christmas. Whether you agree with my conclusions or not, I offer them to you as a place to start your thinking.

Nobody is going to hand you a kinder, gentler, simpler Christmas. If this is what you want, you will have to make it yourself. It's time to reinvent Christmas, again. Maybe we can get it right this time. At least we can try.

CHART YOUR OWN COURSE

Christmas has almost always had a dual nature. Since the earliest days that it was celebrated in Rome on December 25, during a season of pagan merrymaking, it has always been both holy day and holiday, sacred and secular event. After 1,700 years, I do not think we can fundamentally change this situation, so we had better make the best of it. Remember that Christmas will go on with or without Christ, so if we do not bring Christ to Christmas, Christ will not be there.

So it will do no good, as some have suggested, to more widely separate the sacred and secular Christmases, to let the one go its own way while we pursue another way. Such a course will lead only to more confusion and more marginalization of the sacred Christmas. As difficult as it may be to stand against the secular Christmas, we have to remind the secular world what the real Christmas is all about. If truly we believe that Jesus is the reason for the season, we need to give others ample reason to celebrate with us.

A few voices suggest that we should reject most or all Christmas customs in an attempt to keep the season "pure." But rejecting these customs will not get rid of them. It will only put them farther beyond the reach of redemption—and mark those who reject them as cranky contrarians. The harder but wiser course is to reject only those customs that we consider truly unwholesome and work to redeem the rest. By vigorously celebrating their Christian meaning, we can turn these customs more fully to God's glory.

Christmas wars are inevitable because the incarnation of God in Jesus always confronts culture. God is all about redeeming creation, redeeming culture. So the enterprise of turning pagan customs to God's glory is never over, this side of the final establishment of God's kingdom on earth as it is in heaven. Christians are called to be continual witnesses, perpetual martyrs.

Therefore I suggest that we celebrate a fuller Christmas—one that incorporates both the "Holly Jolly Christmas" and the "Joy to the World" Christmas. To do that in your home, you may have to cut back some of the holly and go easy on the jolly. Enjoy the secular Christmas, but do not let the holiday outshine the holy day. Keep your perspective. Remember what you are celebrating. If you can stay centered on Christ, you can add these other things in appropriate measure.

Remember that there is no uncorrupted original that you can return to—at least not one that can be recovered with any confidence. Christmas may always have been a time of conflict and a time of excess as well as a time of hope and joy. But if, indeed, we place Christ at the center of it—as we place Christ at the center of everything in our conflicted lives—then the peace of God that surpasses all understanding will guard our hearts and minds, even in the midst of the conflict.

It may be hard for most of us to imagine today, but celebrating Christmas was illegal in parts of America for more than 20 years. A few extremists may want to make it illegal again, but most people simply want to be left alone to observe it the way they like and not be bothered by those who do it differently.

Let that principle guide you. Focus on what is important to you and ignore the rest. Celebrate Christmas in a way that honors Jesus and uplifts your spirit and does not drive you crazy doing of it. And give others the freedom to go their own way. We should encourage non-Christians to celebrate the secular Christmas in whatever ways they find satisfying. Perhaps if they learn to celebrate the secular Christmas well, they might wonder whether there is more to it than that and be open to hearing about what "more" might be.

At the same time, don't let others steal Christmas from you. Fight for what is yours. The voices of intolerance, both secular and religious, want to muzzle you and force you to follow their way. Don't let them. Know that it is not our government's proper role to promote any one form of religion over another but to keep the public square free for all—and if it is not free for all, it is not free for any.

Stay alert for the lies about Christmas. Remember that much of what you have heard about Christmas is a lie. Christmas is not a pagan holiday. On whatever day we celebrate Jesus' birth, his birth is the only association that hallows the day. Remember that much of what you *will* hear about Christmas is a lie, too. Just as there were those who wanted to seize Jesus to make him their king (John 6:15), so there are those today who want to use Jesus for their own purposes.

Do not concern yourself about the pagan roots of many Christmas customs. Once you were lost. Now you are redeemed. So it is with many of the traditions of Christmas. However they began, we can redeem them. We can turn them to the glory of God, as we ourselves have been turned to God. We were worth saving, or Jesus would not have died for us. Most Christmas customs are worth saving, too, though at considerably less expense.

As much as we may dislike some of the customs we have inherited, and as much as we might sometimes feel burdened by all of them, they do help make Christmas the joyous time it is. We may discover that in throwing some of them out, we may unexpectedly throw the Babe and the manger out with them.

If you no longer feel comfortable with any tradition, drop it and move on, even if this tradition previously gave you joy. Don't be bound by custom but bind custom to your own vision of what Christmas should be. Shape your own celebration from the many possibilities. Be intentional. Don't drift blindly into patterns of behavior. Choose how you will celebrate. Don't try to change everything at once, however. Make little changes each year; they will add up eventually. And always remain open to new possibilities. Always remain open to unexpected movements of the Holy Spirit within you.

Don't let the expectations of others determine how you will celebrate. You know what you want from Christmas. Draw up a plan of how you want to celebrate and fit the wishes and demands of others into it. Compromise when necessary. *Give* when you must, as a gift of love, but don't *give in*. Remember that there are limits to all giving. In the effort to share your celebration of Christmas, don't give away Christmas itself.

Carefully examine your own expectations of Christmas. Don't hope for too much. Don't expect too much of yourself, or of others. Cultivate an attitude of childlike enthusiasm and accept the unexpected.

Seek simplicity and purity of spirit. Christmas is such a busy time of year that it's easy to get lost in the hustle and bustle. It's easy to lose your bearings and focus on the wrong things. Make your celebration as simple as you can and make plenty of room for quiet time. God often speaks softly. You cannot hear God's voice unless you listen in patience. Be quiet and patient and *listen*.

Celebrate *all* of Christmas and celebrate it well. Remember that Christmas is a season, not a single day. The season has a script, a pattern of unfolding. It starts slowly and builds gradually and doesn't end until January 6. Don't jump the gun. Don't celebrate the victory before it is won. Take the parts of the seasons as they come, one by one: Advent, Christmas, Epiphany.

Make Advent your time of preparation. Use this time to prepare for Christmas not just in conventional ways but also in spiritual ways. Let your outer preparations mirror your inner journey. Instead of decorating your home all at once, try adding new decorations day by day, as the time of waiting passes and the time of joy draws closer.

Attend church worship services faithfully. Gather with your brothers and sisters in Christ. Love them and be loved by them. Gather also with your family. Huddle with them around an Advent wreath or home altar and pray earnestly for renewal of Jesus' Spirit within you. Read your Bible and meditate on what it tells you. Sample the vast devotional literature of Christmas and reflect on what it says to you.

Think about what the Incarnation means. Think about God becoming a baby. Think about the Creator of the universe becoming part of creation. Think about the One who "though he was in the form of God, did not regard equality with God as something to be exploited, but emptied himself, taking the form of a slave, being born in human likeness" (Philippians 2:6–7). What kind of love is this?

Accept this love. Rejoice in it. Celebrate it with all your power. And don't let the party die with the sunlight of December 25. Celebrate Christmas for the full Twelve Days. Seek ways of making these days as special as Christmas itself. If you have been decorating your home gradually, perhaps you could save the biggest decorations for last. You might even consider reviving the old custom of waiting to set up the Christmas tree until Christmas Eve. Then on Christmas morning it will still be new and fresh and exciting, and perhaps you will understand, as if for the first time, why it is called the Tree of Life.

Say a prayer or sing a song before you dive into those packages on Christmas morning. Consider not unwrapping all your presents at once but saving some for the days to follow. Don't let the days after Christmas be a letdown. Keep the expectancy and hope alive, for you want them to burn within you long after the season ends. You want to vow with Ebenezer Scrooge: "I will honor Christmas in my heart and try to keep it all the year."

Finally, mark the significance of Epiphany, Jesus' "coming out" party. Don't keep Christmas locked in your heart. Let it out. Let Jesus live in you. In all the world, Jesus has no corporal body except what you give him. Make your body his.

Give as Jesus gave, and not just at Christmas. Don't fall into the gift trap, that complex set of social obligations and unwritten rules that govern so much holiday giving. Write your own rules. Remember that Christmas gifts are only tokens of love. They don't have to be big or elaborate. They have only to be given thoughtfully and lovingly. Draw up a Christmas budget and stick close to it. Make sure your family and friends understand the limits of your Christmas giving. Don't let expectations grow too large.

Don't make gifts the center of a child's Christmas. No gift, no matter how wonderful, can meet all of a child's expectations, so if you focus on gifts, you'll make disappointment inevitable. The anticipation of Christmas will create enough excitement of its own. Pay attention to what counts.

Children may want to make a list for Santa. Go over the list with them, item by item. Discover what things they really would like (and don't be surprised if some of their deepest desires aren't on the list). Determine what things they only *think* they want because they saw a TV commercial for it or they know someone who has it. Trim the list—or rather, let your children trim the list with your guidance. If you keep expectations in line, they will not be disappointed. And if they insist on something that is out of the question as far as you are concerned, tell them simply: "That's a wonderful thing to wish for, but I think it's more than we (or Santa) can provide."

Having curbed their expectations, don't undo your good work by overwhelming children with gifts. And don't let others do it either, even doting grandparents.

Talk about the legend of Saint Nicholas. Let your children understand that all gifts have givers. Encourage them to be givers and set a good example for them. Don't bribe kids with gifts. Make all gifts as unconditional as your love. Be a loving Santa, and create new loving Santas.

Above all, surround your children with love. Make them your Christkindl and love Christ through them with acts of kindness and understanding. When children know that they are loved, they do not feel disappointed when they don't get exactly the gift they wanted. Your love is more important to them than any gift you could wrap in colorful paper and top with a bow.

Give unselfishly to others, too. Don't feel *obliged* to give tips to your hairdresser or bonuses to your employees. But feel *free* to give to them, to show your appreciation for them as fellow human beings. Be especially mindful of those who cannot reward you or even offer you their thanks. Make whatever contributions to charity that you can afford. This is a line item in your Christmas budget, not a part of "miscellaneous." Make it a priority, within your limits. If you cannot give money, give time.

And don't stop giving when the Christmas season is over. Giving should be as great a part of your life as receiving. From what you have received, freely give. It's not yours anyway. You only got it on loan from God. Give thanks to God for all that you have and all that you can give to others. Give thanks especially for God's Son, whose love alone gives meaning to all our shallow observances.

If you approach Christmas in this way, yours can be a merry holiday, and a blessed holy day, too. Like Ebenezer Scrooge, you will have learned how to keep Christmas well.

Endnotes

1. "Black Christmas."
2. Boorstin, *The Americans,* 159.
3. "Holiday and Seasonal Trends."
4. "Quick Tree Facts."
5. "Holiday Mail."
6. Kavilanz, "Trashy Christmas."
7. Henry, "Why I Hate Christmas."
8. Waldfogel, *Scroogenomics*; Will, "Christmas giving."
9. Volf, "One-way giving."
10. McKibben, "Christmas unplugged."
11. Quoted in Buchanan, "Christmastide."
12. "Overland Park Man"; "Man Outraged," "Zoo Statures"; "Complaint."
13. Origen. *Commentary on Matthew*, 10.11.
14. Eldersheim, *Life and Times*, 131.
15. Roll, *Origins*, 84.
16. Talley, *Origins*, 135-36.
17. Cullman, "Origin," 33.
18. Talley, *Origins*, 86–87.
19. Roll, *Origins*, 86.
20. Clement, *Stromata*, 1.21.45.

21. Talley, *Origins*, 96–97, citing Augustine, *On the Trinity* 4.5.
22. Talley, *Origins*, 8.
23. Talley, "Afterthoughts," 4.
24. Cullman, "Early Church," 27.
25. Cullman, "Early Church," 27–28.
26. Roll, *Origins*, 66–67.
27. Talley, "*Origins*," 103–106, citing Epiphanius, *Panarion* 51.22.3.
28. MacMullen, *Christianity and Paganism*, 155.
29. Crossan, *God & Empire*, 147–48.
30. Roll, *Origins*, 150, 174.
31. Talley, *Origins*, 95.
32. Cullman, "Early Church," 36.
33. Leo, *Nativity*.
34. Augustine, *On Christian Doctrine* 40.
35. Chadwick, *Early Church*, 168.
36. Jerome, *Epistle* 58.
37. Bahat, "Jesus' Tomb," 181.
38. Bede, *History* 1.30.
39. Chadwick, *Early Church*, 126, 128–29.
40. Tertullian, *On Idolatry* 15.
41. Del Re, *Almanack*, 23.
42. Miles, *Christmas Customs*, 168.
43. Wedgeworth, "Halloween."
44. "Holiday and Seasonal Trends."
45. Del Re, *Almanack*, 22.
46. Nissenbaum, *Battle*.
47. Forbes, *Candid History*, 64.

48. Restad, *Christmas in America*, 105; Forbes, *Candid History*, 60–66; Gillis, *Their Own Making*, 98–102; Golby and Purdue, *Modern Christmas*, 14–18.
49. Restad, *Christmas in America*, 14.
50. Restad, *Christmas in America*, 30–31; Nissenbaum, *Battle*, 4, 36.
51. St. James, *Simplify*, 10.
52. "Holiday and Seasonal Trends."
53. "Christmas Wars," 12–13; Simon, "Save Christmas."
54. Goldberg, "Secular Humanist Grinch;" Stack, "War on Christmas;" Denvir, "A Short History."
55. Pavlovitz, "There Is a War"; Pavlovitz, "There Is No War."
56. The date, wording, and meaning of the saying are disputed. This version comes from https://www.dwightdeisenhower.com/193/Religion.
57. Neuhaus, *Naked Square*.

Bibliography

Auld, William Muir. *Christmas Traditions*. New York: Macmillan, 1931.
Bahat, Dan. "The Holy Sepulchre Church—Jesus' Tomb." In Hershel Shanks, ed., *Where Christianity Was Born*, 176–195. Washington: Biblical Archaeological Society, 2006.
Bennett, William J. *The True Saint Nicholas: Why He Matters to Christmas*. New York: Howard, 2009.
Boorstin, Daniel J. *The Americans: The Democratic Experience*. New York: Vintage, 1974.
Bowler, Gerry. *Christmas in the Crosshairs*. Oxford: Oxford University Press, 2017.
Buchanan, John M. "Christmastide." *Christian Century*, December 25, 2007. https://www.christiancentury.org/article/2007-12/christmastide.
"Complaint about Buddha Statues at Kansas City Zoo Is Off." *St. Louis Today*. https://www.stltoday.com/news/local/complaint-about-buddha-statues-at-kansas-city-zoo-is-off/article_2e4e033f-7428-5a60-ad38-171ac2977d69.html.
Chadwick, Henry. *The Early Church*. New York: Pelican, 1967.
Christie, Judy. *Hurry Less, Worry Less at Christmastime*. Nashville: Abingdon, 2011.
"Christmas Wars Enrich Some Advocacy Groups." *Christian Century*. January 9, 2007.
Clapp, Rodney. "The Numbing Season." *Christian Century*, December. 14, 2010.
Cline, Austin. "Christmas Wars & Conspiracies: Conflicts Over the Meaning of the Christmas Season." December 11, 2005, *about.com*. No longer online.
Cooke, Gillian, ed. *A Celebration of Christmas*. New York: Putnam, 1980.
Corcoran, Mary E. "This Year, Give Children a Most-Wanted Gift—Your Time." *Kansas City Times*, December 15, 1987.
Crippen, T. G. *Christmas and Christmas Lore*. London: Blackie, 1923.
Crossan, John Dominic. *God & Empire*. New York: HarperOne, 2007.
Cullman, Oscar. "The Origin of Christmas." In *The Early Church*, 21–36. Philadelphia: Westminster, 1956.
Dawson, W. F. *Christmas: Its Origins and Associations*. London: Stock, 1902.
Del Re, Gerard and Patricia. *The Christmas Almanack*. Garden City: Doubleday, 1979.
Denvir, Daniel. "A Short History of the War on Christmas." *Politico*, December 16, 2013. https://www.politico.com/magazine/story/2013/12/war-on-christmas-short-history-101222.
"Dreaming of a Black Christmas." *The Economist*. November 27. 2008. www.economist.com/business/2008/11/27/dreaming-of-a-black-christmas.
Duncan, David Ewing. *Calendar: Humanity's Epic Struggle to Determine a True and Accurate Year*. New York: Morrow, 1998.
Edworthy, Niall. *The Curious World of Christmas*. New York: Pelican-Perigee, 2007.

Bibliography

Eldersheim, Alfred. *The Life and Times of Jesus the Messiah*, Peabody: Hendrickson, 1993.
Elliott, Jock. *Inventing Christmas: How Our Holiday Came to Be*. New York: Abrams, 2002.
Emerson, Ralph Waldo. "Gifts," *Essays: Second Series*. 1844.
Evans, G. R. *The Thought of Gregory the Great*. Cambridge: Cambridge University Press, 1986.
Flanders, Judith. *Christmas: A Biography*. New York: St. Martin's, 2017.
Flynn, Tom. *The Trouble With Christmas*. Buffalo: Prometheus, 1993.
Forbes, Bruce David. *Christmas: A Candid History*. Berkeley: University of California Press, 2007.
Gibbs, Nancy. "America's Holy War." *Time*, December 9, 1991.
Giblin, James Cross. *The Truth About Santa Claus*. New York: Crowell, 1985.
Gibson, John. *The War on Christmas: How the Liberal Plot to Ban the Sacred Holiday Is Worse Than You Thought*. New York: Sentinel, 2006.
Gillis, John R. *A World of Their Own Making*. New York: Basic, 1996.
Goldberg, Michelle. "How the Secular Humanist Grinch Didn't Steal Christmas." *Salon*, November 21, 2005. https://www.salon.com/2005/11/21/christmas_6/.
Golby, J. M. and A. W. Purdue. *The Making of the Modern Christmas*. Atlanta: University of Georgia Press, 1986.
Goodman, Ellen. "Gift Giving is More About Relationships Than Gifts." clipping from unknown newspaper dated December 26, 2002.
Gordon, T. David. "The Decline of Christianity in the West? A Contrarian View." *Ordained Servant*, Vol. 16, 2007. https://opc.org/os.html?article_id=44.
Greeley, Andrew W. "Christmas Without the Trappings Is No Christmas at All." *Religion News Service*, December 14, 1994.
Hadfield, Miles and John. *The Twelve Days of Christmas*. New York: Little, Brown, 1961.
Heinz, Donald. *Christmas: Festival of Incarnation*. Minneapolis: Fortress, 2010.
Henry, James S. "Why I Hate Christmas." *New Republic*, December 31, 1990, 21–24.
Hickman, Hoyt, et al. *The New Handbook of the Christian Year*. Nashville: Abingdon, 1992.
Hijmans, Steven. "Sol Invictus, the Winter Solstice and the Origins of Christmas." *Mouseion: Journal of the Classical Association of Canada*, Series 3 Vol. 3 (2003) 377–98.
"Holiday and Seasonal Trends." *National Retail Federation*. https://nrf.com/insights/holiday-and-seasonal-trends.
Hottes, Alfred Carl. *1001 Christmas Facts and Fancies*. New York: DeLaMare, 1937.
"Is Santa a Deadweight Loss?" *The Economist*. December 20, 2001. tps://www.economist.com/christmas-specials/2001/12/20/is-santa-a-deadweight-loss.
Jones, Charles W. *Saint Nicholas of Myra, Bari and Manhattan: Biography of a Legend*. Chicago, University of Chicago Press, 1978.
Jones, Cheslyn, et al., eds. *The Study of Liturgy*. London: Oxford University Press, 1992.
Kavilanz. Parija. "Dreaming of a Trashy Christmas." *CNN Money*, December 17, 2010. https://money.cnn.com/2010/12/16/news/economy/holiday_trash/index.htm
Kelly, Joseph F. *The Origins of Christmas*. Collegeville: Liturgical, 2004.
Klauer, Theodor. *A Short History of the Western Liturgy*. Oxford: Oxford University Press, 1979.
Krythe, Mayme R. *All About Christmas*. New York: Harper, 1954.
Lawhead, Alice Slaikeu. *The Christmas Survival Book*. Batavia: Lion, 1985.
Leo I. *On the Feast of the Nativity II*, Sermon 22, part VI.
Levine, Deborah J. "The December dilemma." *Christian Century*, December 15, 1993.

Bibliography

Lizorkin-Eyzenberg, Eli. "Is Christmas a Pagan Holiday?" *Israeli Bible Center,* December 20, 2018. https://weekly.israelbiblecenter.com/christmas-pagan-holiday/.
Lubin, Leonard B. *Christmas Gift-Bringers.* New York: Shepard, 1989.
MacBeth, Sybil. *The Season of Nativity.* Brewster: Paraclete, 2014.
MacMullen, Ramsay. *Christianity and Paganisn in the Fourth to the Eighth Centuries.* New Haven: Yale University Press, 1997.
"Man Outraged by Zoo's Buddha Statues." *United Press International.* https://www.upi.com/Odd_News/2009/01/14/Man-outraged-by-zoos-Buddha-statues/92311231983772/.
Marling, Karal Ann. *Merry Christmas! Celebrating America's Greatest Holiday.* Cambridge: Harvard University Press, 2000.
McGowan, Andrew. "How December 25 Became Christmas." *Bible History Daily,* December 7, 2012. https://www.biblicalarchaeology.org/daily/people-cultures-in-the-bible/jesus-historical-jesus/how-december-25-became-christmas/.
McKibben, Bill. "Christmas Unplugged." *Christianity Today,* December 9, 1996.
———. *Hundred Dollar Holiday: The Case for a More Joyful Christmas.* New York: Simon & Schuster, 1998.
McKinley, Rick, et al. *Advent Conspiracy.* Grand Rapids: Zondervan, 2009.
Miles, Clement A. *Christmas Customs and Traditions: Their History and Significance.* New York: Dover, 1976.
Nardone, Richard M. *The Story of the Christian Year.* New York: Paulist, 1991.
Neuhaus, Richard John. *The Naked Public Square: Religion and Democracy in America.* Grand Rapids: Eerdmans, 1986.
Nissenbaum, Stephen. *The Battle for Christmas.* New York: Knopf, 1996.
Nothaft, C. P. E. "The Origins of the Christmas Date: Some Recent Trends in Historical Research." Church History 81, no. 4 (2012): 903-11. http://www.jstor.org/stable/23358685.
Ostling, Richard. "Why Is December 25 the Date to Celebrate Christmas?" Associated Press dispatch. *Kansas City Star.* December 25, 2005.
"Overland Park Man Complains About Zoo's Buddha statues." *Kansas City Star.* January 13, 2009, electronic edition. No longer online.
Palin, Sarah. *Good Tidings and Great Joy: Protecting the Heart of Christmas.* New York: Broadside, 2013.
Pavlovitz, John. "No Christians, There is No War on Christmas." December 15, 2016, *johnpavlotitz.com.*
———. "Yes, There is a War on Christmas." November 24, 2018, *johnpavlotitz.com.*
Peluso-Verdend, Gary. "Christians Have Lost the War for Christmas." *President's Greeting.* Phillips Seminary, October 1, 2017, *ptstulsa.edu.* No longer online.
"Quick Tree Facts." National Christmas Tree Foundation. http://www.realchristmastrees.org/dnn/Education/Quick-Tree-Facts.
Ramsland, Marcia. *Simplify Your Holidays.* Nashville: Nelson, 2008.
Ratcliff, Robert A. "Three Old Sinners, Just Like Us." *Ministry Matters.com,* December 26, 2012. https://www.ministrymatters.com/all/entry/3464/three-old-sinners-just-like-us.
Restad, Penne L. *Christmas in America: A History.* New York: Oxford, 1995.
Richards, Katharine Lambert. *How Christmas Came to the Sunday-School.* New York: Dodd, Mead, 1934.
Rifkin, Jeremy. *Time Wars.* New York: Simon & Schuster, 1987.

Bibliography

Robinson, Jo and Jean Coppock Staeheli. U*nplug the Christmas Machine: How to Have the Christmas You've Always Wanted.* New York: Morrow, 1982.

Roll, Susan K. *Toward the Origins of Christmas*. Kampen, Netherlands: Kok Pharos, 1995.

St. James, Elaine. *Simplify Your Christmas*. Kansas City: Andrews McMeel, 1998.

Sachs, Andrea. "Why We Shouldn't Give Christmas Gifts." *Time*, November 12, 2009. http://content.time.com/time/business/article/0,8599,1938367,00.html.

Shelley, Bruce L. "Is Christmas Pagan?" *Christianity Today*, December 6, 1999.

Simcoe, Mary Ann, ed. *A Christmas Sourcebook*. Chicago: Liturgy Training, 1984.

Simmons, Kurt. "Revisiting the Fathers: An Examination of the Christmas Date in Several Early Patristic Writers," *Questions Liturgiques/Studies in Liturgy* 98 (2017) 143–80.

Simon, Stephanie. "Save Christmas: Send Money." *Los Angeles Times*, December 23, 2006; https://www.latimes.com/archives/la-xpm-2006-dec-23-na-christmas23-story.html.

Slaughter, Mike. *Christmas Is Not Your Birthday*. Nashville: Abingdon, 2011.

Snyder, Phillips. *December 25th: The Joys of Christmas Past*. New York: Dodd, Mead, 1985.

Stack, Liam. "How the 'War on Christmas' Controversy Was Created." *New York Times*, December 19, 2006. https://www.nytimes.com/2016/12/19/us/war-on-christmas-controversy.html.

Stevens, Patricia Bunning. *Merry Christmas: A History of the Holiday*. New York: Macmillan, 1979.

Stookey, Laurence Hull. *Calendar: Christ's Time for the Church*. Nashville: Abingdon, 1996.

Talley, Thomas J. *The Origins of the Liturgical Year*. New York: Pueblo, 1986.

———. "Afterthoughts on 'The Origins of the Liturgical Year.' " In *Western Plainchant in the First Millennium*, 1–10. Edited by Sean Gallagher, et al. Aldershot: Ashgate, 2003.

Tighe, William J. "Calculating Christmas: The Story Behind December 25." *Touchstone*, December 2003. https://www.touchstonemag.com/archives/article.php?id=16-10-012-v.

"Holiday Mail Volume Expected to Hit 20 Billion." *USPS*. November 21, 2007. https://uspsblog.com/holiday-shipping-stats/.

Volf, Miroslav. "One-way Giving." *Christian Century*, December 27, 2003, 31.

———. "The Giver and the Gift." *Christian Century*, January 6, 2016, 10–11.

Waldfogel, Joel. *Scroogenomics: Why You Shouldn't Buy Presents for the Holidays*. Princeton, N.J.: Princeton University Press, 2009.

Wedgeworth, Steven. "Halloween: Its Creation and Recreation." October 30, 2013, *calvinistinternational.com*.

Weiser, Francis X. *The Christmas Book*. New York: Harcourt, Brace, 1952.

Wernecke, Herbert H. *Christmas Customs Around the World*. Philadelphia: Westminster, 1975.

White, James F. *Introduction to Christian Worship*. Nashville: Abingdon, 1990.

Will, George F. "George F. Will on the Disaster of Christmas Giving." *The Washington Post*, November 26, 2009; http://www.washingtonpost.com/wp-dyn/content/article/2009/11/25/AR2009112502653.html.

"Zoo Statues Not Buddhas." *United Press International*. https://www.upi.com/Odd_News/2009/01/15/Zoo-statues-not-Buddhas/30431232053590/.

www.ingramcontent.com/pod-product-compliance
Lightning Source LLC
Chambersburg PA
CBHW070453090426
42735CB00012B/2534